Plains Apache Ethnobotany

Plains Apache girls, 1901. Connie May, age 13 or 14, on right. Courtesy of the Western History Collection, University of Oklahoma Libraries.

Plains Apache Ethnobotany

Julia A. Jordan

Foreword by Paul E. Minnis and Wayne J. Elisens

University of Oklahoma Press : Norman

All photographs are by Julia A. Jordan unless otherwise indicated.

Library of Congress Cataloging-in-Publication Data

Jordan, Julia A., 1928–
    Plains Apache ethnobotany / Julia A. Jordan ; foreword by Paul E. Minnis and
Wayne J. Elisens.
        p.   cm.
    Includes bibliographical references and index.
    ISBN 978-0-8061-3968-5 (hardcover) ISBN 978-0-8061-9401-1 (paper)
    1. Apache Indians—Medicine. 2. Traditional medicine—Great Plains. 3. Medicinal
plants—Great Plains. 4. Plants—Religious aspects. 5. Ethnobotany—Great Plains. 4.
Plants—Religious aspects. 5. Ethnobotany—Great Plains. 6. Human-plant relation-
ships—Great Plains. 7. Apache Indians—Social life and customs. 8. Great Plains—
Social life and customs. I. Title.
    E99.A6J67 2008
    979.004'9725—dc22

2008015458

Copyright © 2008 by the University of Oklahoma Press, Norman, Publishing Division
of the University. Paperback published 2024. Manufactured in the U.S.A.

In memory of
William E. Bittle
Fred Bigman
Ray Blackbear
Gertrude Chalepah
Rose Chaletsin
Connie May (Datose) Saddleblanket
Louise (Susagossa) Saddleblanket

These things should be passed on, according to my notion. To the grave with us is no place for it. Our young peoples should know of our language, belief, and history, of our generation. It should be put in writing.

Ray Blackbear, July 6, 1961

Contents

Illustrations

PHOTOGRAPHS

MAP

Tables

Foreword

Perhaps the most common image of American Indians is the horse-mounted bison hunter of the Great Plains, bow ready to bring down an animal that supplied nearly all the needs of the hunter. Among other limitations, this icon devalues the importance of plants to indigenous peoples of the plains. They used plants to provide many services, such as food, medicines, rituals, shelter, and other material needs. Furthermore, among American Indians, plants often have symbolic importance that transcends their material utility. Daniel E. Moerman's encyclopedic volume *Native American Ethnobotany* (1998) enumerates nearly three thousand species of plants used by the indigenous peoples of North America, with food and medicines being the most common plant uses by far. While Moerman's compendium does not divide plant uses by region, several hundred of these plants are natives of the Great Plains.

The importance of plants for Plains Indians really should not surprise us, as this region has a rich biotic and cultural diversity. The midcontinent prairies and steppes of North America cover a large area and encompass at least five distinct ecoregion provinces (Bailey et al. 1994). Mixed-grass and short-grass prairies, the predominant vegetation of the current homeland of the Plains Apache, originally covered nearly 120 million hectares in the United States (Sims and Risser 2000). Despite the too popular image of the Great Plains as monotonous grasslands, there is substantial environmental diversity, with over three thousand plant species (Great Plains Flora Association 1986) and a diversity of vegetation types (Küchler 1964).

Within the Great Plains, the Apache Tribe of Oklahoma is located in an area of exceptional ecological diversity. Although much of this area lies within gently rolling redbed plains with characteristic sand- and clay-based soils (Curtis et al. 1972), topographical and substrate diversity is enhanced by limestone hills and the granitic uplift comprising the Wichita Mountains, rising to an elevation of 2,464 feet (751 meters) at Mount Scott. Reflecting this environmental diversity, the three-county area (Caddo, Comanche, and Kiowa counties) where most Plains Apache currently reside has over twelve hundred vascular plant species, representing at least 115 plant families (Hoagland et al. 2004). The vegetation of this region within Oklahoma is equally varied, with five distinct grassland plant communities, post oak–blackjack oak forests (the Cross Timbers), and riverine woodlands (Bruner 1931; Hoagland 2000). The Plains Apache utilized a wide variety of plants from all of the major habitats.

Matching the biotic diversity of the Great Plains is the region's cultural diversity. Numerous indigenous groups called the plains home (DeMallie 2001). Each developed their own unique lifeways based on a range of economic strategies that combined hunting, gathering, raiding, and trading. Some, like the Mandan, were farmers who lived much of the year in substantial villages, while others, such as the Plains Apache, relied most heavily on hunting and gathering. The diversity was not based solely on the numbers of American Indian groups but also on their changing lifestyles. The introduction of the horse, gun, and markets as well as political and demographic pressure from the expanding United States altered Plains Indians and their neighbors, changes well documented in the historical record.

The study of plains ethnobotany stretches back over a century. Exact figures are hard to find, but Ford (1978: 37) cataloged ethnobotanical reports for North America from before 1896 through 1977. The plains accounted for 87 reports, second only behind the American Southwest ($n = 195$) and slightly more than the Northeast ($n = 84$). Included are some classics of American Indian ethnobotany, including some pioneering studies of American Indian agriculture (e.g., Blankinship 1905; Gilmore 1919; Prescott 1849; Wilson 1917) complemented by ethnobotanical information in early ethnographies of plains groups (e.g., Grinnell 1923). Many of these classic studies are from the northern plains. Less well represented is the ethnobotany of the southern plains, although there are exceptions, including the immediate neighbors of the Plains

Apache with whom they shared a reservation from 1867 to 1901, the Kiowa (Vestal and Schultes 1939) and the Comanche (Carlson and Jones 1940; Jones 1968).

Julia Jordan's book is a valuable contribution in several ways, and we are pleased that it will reach the wide audience that it has long deserved. She has documented more plant species used by a people native to the southern plains and has utilized a greater number of informants than previous ethnobotanical studies in this region, and she is also the first to include information provided by both male and female elders. Included in her book is a wealth of cultural information and detailed descriptions concerning the selection, preparation, and use of over one hundred species of native plants by the Plains Apache. While the book's core is her master's thesis, she also presents some new information.

The relevance of her observations has only increased over the years. Much of the information gathered by Jordan cannot be replicated today. The Plains Apaches who worked with Jordan were elders in the 1960s, individuals who were raised at a critical time, balanced between a more traditional lifeway and greater involvement in a market economy and modern political realities. The fact that Jordan's thesis is being published more than forty years after its completion rather than sitting on a dusty shelf is a clear testament to its quality and significance to the Plains Apache, to the people of Oklahoma, and to those interested in the use of plants.

This book helps fill a vacuum in two ways. First, ethnobotanical information for the Plains Apache's closest neighbors, the Kiowa and Comanche, is widely available, so publication of this volume fills in a void for southwestern Oklahoma. One could argue that these data have been available since the 1960s. However, the fact that Jordan's information is not in Moerman's encyclopedia of American Indian plant use indicates how important the publication of this book is for disseminating its information and insights.

Second, plant use information is available for many other Apache groups, including the Chiricahua, Mescalero, Western, San Carlos, and White Mountain (see Moerman 1998 for bibliographic summary), so substantial information about Plains Apache ethnobotany is most welcome, especially in light of the fact that the Plains Apache inhabit a plant world quite different from their cousins in the American Southwest. This helps us understand the role that environment, culture, and history plays in plant use.

When viewed though a wider lens, this work documents the world of the largely hunting-gathering Plains Apache. Most ethnobotanical information on the Great Plains is for farming groups, so an expanded understanding of plains hunting and gathering is important to appreciate modern history as well as to know better the lives of ancient hunting and gathering peoples who inhabited the plains for many prehistoric millennia.

We have emphasized the intricate relationships between the Plains Apache and the environmental milieu of the Great Plains, especially of southwest Oklahoma. However, even when people are rooted in a region, they are rarely limited to a small location. As Jordan discusses, the Plains Apache had and continue to have enduring relationships with other Apache communities in the American Southwest and with non-Apache groups both inside and outside of Oklahoma. The relationship with other American Indian groups is especially interesting in light of the unique history of Indian Territory and the state of Oklahoma, where many tribes were brought together. Therefore, the salient landscape of the Plains Apache is quite wide in terms of geography, history, and culture contacts.

Jordan's Plains Apache collaborators may no longer be with us, but their legacy is now more conveniently shared with their descendants and others respectfully interested in plant use.

Paul E. Minnis and Wayne J. Elisens

Preface and Acknowledgments

Seldom in life is one presented with the opportunity to update and bring to public awareness the results of research conducted decades ago. That such an opportunity has come to me at this time in my life is something of a miracle. I am sincerely grateful for the chance to bring to fruition a dream long cherished and long hoped for—that is, the publication of a revised, expanded, and updated version of my master's thesis, "Ethnobotany of the Kiowa Apache," completed in 1965 for the Department of Anthropology, University of Oklahoma.

The ethnobotany is based primarily upon fieldwork done in the summers of 1963 and 1964, when I was a participant in the University of Oklahoma's Field Schools in Ethnology and Linguistics, headquartered in Anadarko, Oklahoma. These field schools, as well as others conducted in the summers of 1961 and 1965, were funded by the National Science Foundation and directed by Dr. William E. Bittle, professor of anthropology at the University of Oklahoma. They had the double purpose of introducing graduate students in anthropology to fieldwork with American Indians and recovering information on the traditional way of life of a particular group, the Kiowa Apache, referred to hereafter in this book as the Plains Apache. The Plains Apache were asked to assist with the field schools because Dr. Bittle had for some years had excellent relations with this community and several of their elders were anxious that their history and traditions be written down and preserved for the benefit of future generations.

The idea that I should focus on ethnobotany was suggested by Dr. Bittle, who was my academic advisor in graduate studies. The idea was

compatible with my own long-standing interest in the history and ethnology of American Indian peoples of the Great Plains and also with my
love of native plants. I readily accepted his suggestion, and the result
was my master's thesis.

Although I did not continue ethnobotanical research beyond my
thesis, I continued to visit and interact with Plains Apache friends during
my later work as a research anthropologist on other projects at the University of Oklahoma. I did extensive fieldwork for the Doris Duke Indian
Oral History Project, collecting and organizing oral history materials
from American Indian elders in Oklahoma. At the Sam Noble Oklahoma
Museum of Natural History, I served as consultant and co-principal
investigator on several anthropological projects in which Plains Apache
people were active participants. As enduring as my professional interests
and equally important to me have been my close relationships with my
Plains Apache friends. I hope that they and future generations of their
families find this book helpful.

Over the years I have learned that a number of people have accessed
the thesis and found it useful for various research purposes. But the real
impetus to prepare the study for publication came recently, when anthropologist and ethnobotanist Paul Minnis and botanist Wayne Elisens
again expressed interest in the work and encouraged me to prepare it for
possible publication. The present work encompasses the original thesis,
which has been substantially modified in the following respects.

First, I have expanded the section on Plains Apache history and traditional culture to provide a fuller appreciation of the ethnobotanical
data. Although considerable literature on the Plains Apache (also called
Kiowa Apache) exists, most of it is contained in specialized anthropological publications, theses, and dissertations that can be difficult for
many readers to access. The historical review explains that the Plains
Apache were residents of the plains since at least the early 1500s and
were therefore well acquainted with the native flora of the region. They
had no tradition or memory of ever having practiced horticulture. Thus,
this ethnobotany is that of hunter-gatherers, long-time residents of the
plains with no background of a horticultural way of life.

Second, I have revised the discussions of certain plants, most notably
the junipers (*Juniperus* sp.), so as to include materials not available to me

in 1965. I have also added several plants to the inventory of culturally significant plants. These include black walnut (*Juglans nigra*) and a plant used for personal adornment, mescal bean (*Sophora secundiflora*), both of which I had inadvertently omitted in my thesis. Plants that I have become acquainted with since 1965 have also been added. These include frosted mint, or White Sands sage (*Poliomintha incana*), which I first saw in 1967 when I accompanied several Apache friends to the Mescalero Apache Reservation in New Mexico. Most exciting to me was the identification in early 2007 of two important ritual plants, Porter's licoriceroot, or osha, (*Ligusticum porteri*) and Pinchot's juniper, or redberry juniper (*Juniperus pinchotii*). I have added discussion of all of these plants to the ethnobotanical chapters.

Third, both the scientific and common names of the plants have been updated by Wayne Elisens and Richard Thomas of the Oklahoma Biological Survey so that they conform to the current nomenclature of the United States Department of Agriculture (USDA) PLANTS Database. The new terms have been cross-referenced to the former terms in the text and in the index. Also, two tables summarizing information on the vascular plants known to have been used by the Plains Apache have been added.

Fourth, I have identified the Plains Apache elders who provided the ethnobotanical data by their real names, which is the currently accepted practice in most anthropological studies. (In my thesis I had used initials.) I have added brief biographical sketches of the elders, as well as comments on the nature of our interactions during and after the fieldwork.

Finally, I have reordered and reworked some parts of the ethnobotanical chapters to clarify some passages and ensure continuity of thought. Also, the passages dealing with anthropological theory, which graduate students normally include for the benefit of their thesis committee members, have been eliminated.

In preparing this manuscript for publication I have had to revisit in thought and memory those wonderful years spent in close association with the Plains Apache people, with Dr. Bittle, and with my graduate student friends. The elders who shared their knowledge of plants are long deceased, but I am pleased to say that some of their descendants are still my close friends. I also came to realize that it was the fervent desire of the Plains Apache elders, and of Dr. Bittle, that this ethnobotany be completed and published. I am grateful for the opportunity to comply with their wishes. I have made my best effort to interpret correctly the materials available to me, but if there are errors, they are my own.

I am greatly indebted to Dr. Paul E. Minnis of the Anthropology Department of the University of Oklahoma for encouraging me to revitalize my thesis manuscript and prepare it for publication. I deeply appreciate his careful review and critique of the text, as well as his thoughtful advice and suggestions. I am indebted also to Dr. Wayne J. Elisens, professor of botany and curator of the Robert Bebb Herbarium of the University of Oklahoma, for his interest in the Plains Apache ethnobotany, for his updating of the scientific names, for providing a map of the Plains Apache territory in Oklahoma, for his permission to use his tables on vascular plants used by the Plains Apache, and for many other contributions to the botanical aspects of this work.

I wish to thank Dr. Sean O'Neill of the Anthropology Department of the University of Oklahoma, Dr. Mary Linn, curator of linguistics at the Sam Noble Oklahoma Museum of Natural History, and Dr. John Dunn, professor emeritus of linguistics at the University of Oklahoma, for their assistance in locating and using fonts suitable for inserting Plains Apache language terms into the text.

I also extend profound thanks to the reviewers of this manuscript: Dr. Kelly Kindscher, associate scientist of the Kansas Biological Survey; and Dr. Richard I. Ford, professor emeritus of anthropology and curator of ethnology and ethnobotany at the University of Michigan Museum of Anthropology. Both reviewers provided many useful comments and constructive suggestions.

I also acknowledge the help of two other persons from the Sam Noble Oklahoma Museum of Natural History: Dr. Don Wyckoff, professor of anthropology and curator of archaeology, for locating certain reference materials and for his overall encouragement and support; and Dr. Dan Swan, curator of ethnology, for reviewing the material on *Lophophora williamsii* (peyote) and discussing Plains Apache history with me.

I thank the National Science Foundation for funding the University of Oklahoma Field Schools in Ethnology and Linguistics of 1961, 1963, 1964, and 1965 and the Western History Collection of the University of Oklahoma Libraries for permission to use a photograph of Plains Apache elder Connie May Saddleblanket. I also want to thank Patricia Heinicke, Jr., for her careful editing in preparing the manuscript for publication.

Finally, I express my deepest gratitude to members of the Apache Tribe of Oklahoma, the Plains Apache people, whose friendship, wisdom, and willingness to share some of their traditional knowledge have made this work possible.

Note on Orthography and Pronunciation

The Plains Apache terms used in the book were recorded in the field seasons of 1963 and 1964 with the orthography used by Dr. Harry Hoijer (1938). All of the terms were either recorded or reviewed by William Bittle, linguist and professor of anthropology at the University of Oklahoma. The terms presented here are phonemic transcriptions, and the translations are approximate renditions of the meanings provided by the Apache elders.

I have not the expertise to conduct and include a detailed linguistic analysis of the Apache terms. However, I feel that the terms, which were accurate phonemic transcriptions, should be included in this ethnobotany. They reveal certain important Plains Apache concepts of the plant world, as well as provide names and descriptions of culturally significant plants. Furthermore, the terms may be of interest not only to ethnobotanists and specialists in Apachean languages but to members of the Apache Tribe of Oklahoma, many of whom have made an effort to study their language.

With the guidance of Dr. Bittle, I used Dr. Hoijer's orthography in my fieldwork and in writing my master's thesis, "Ethnobotany of the Kiowa Apache," which was completed in 1965 at the University of Oklahoma. At that time, special characters and diacritical marks could be inserted into a thesis text by hand. However, for practical purposes, I am using a modification of Dr. Hoijer's system. This modification allows me to use a Times New Roman Navajo font for all of the Apache characters except the voiced velar spirant, which I prefer to represent by the Latin small letter gamma (γ) rather than the English consonant cluster *gh*.

The Plains Apache consonants *b, d, g, h, k, l, m, n, s, t, y,* and *z* have essentially the same pronunciation as their English equivalents. Other Apache consonants, along with Hoijer's original and modified orthography and suggestions for pronunciation, are given in the table below.

Hoijer Orthography		Description and Pronunciation Suggestions
Original	Modified	
ȝ	dz	Voiced alveolar affricate, as in English *adze*
c	ts	Voiceless alveolar affricate, as in German *zeit*
ł	ł	Voiceless alveolar lateral, similar to *ll* in Welch *Llwyd*
λ	dl	Voiced lateral affricate, almost like the *dl* in *gladly*
ƛ	tł	Voiceless lateral affricate, as in Nahuatl *tlaloc*
š	sh	Voiceless alveolar spirant, as in English *shell*
ž	zh	Voiced alveolar spirant, as in English *azure*
ǯ	j	Voiced alveolar affricate, as in English *jet*
č	ch	Voiceless alveolar affricate, as in English *church*
x	x	Voiceless velar spirant, as in Scottish *loch*
γ	γ	Voiced velar spirant, a very soft *g* with aspiration
ʔ	'	Glottal stop, as in English *uh-oh*

Some consonants may be glottalized; in this work these are written as *t', ts', tł', ch',* and *k'.*

The Plains Apache vowels are: *a, e, i,* and *o.* They may be long or short; they may be nasalized; and there are four possible tones for each vowel. Short vowels are here written as single letters, whereas long vowels are written as double letters. Nasalization is indicated by a subscript hook. Vowel tones are indicated as follows: high tone is indicated by an acute accent; low tone is indicated by lack of an accent. Long vowels may have rising tone or falling tone; one of the double letters carries an acute accent to indicate the higher tone. Here are some examples of Plains Apache vowels: *a* (short, low tone), *á* (short, high tone), *ą* (short, low tone, nasalized), *ą́* (short, high tone, nasalized), *aa* (long, low tone), *áá* (long, high tone), *ąą* (long, nasalized), *ą́ą́* (long, high tone, nasalized), *aá* (long, rising tone), *áa* (long, falling tone), *ąą́* (long, rising tone, nasalized), and *ą́ą* (long, falling tone, nasalized).

Vowel pronunciation is as follows:

a	as in German *mann*
aa	as in English *father*
e	as in English *bet*
ee	as in English *bed*
i	varies from sound of English *bid* to that of English *beat*
ii	as in English *bead*
o	varies from sound of German *so* to that of English *boot*
oo	varies from sound of German *Sohn* to that of English *sooth*

More information on the Plains Apache language may be found in papers by Bittle (1956, 1963) and Hoijer (1938, 1971). In these papers the language is referred to as "Kiowa Apache."

Plains Apache Ethnobotany

Introduction

Clusters of multi-trunked, irregularly shaped junipers grow on a low, limestone mountain in Kiowa County in western Oklahoma. Their dark-green branches stand out in stark contrast against a clear and unpolluted blue sky. It is June of 2007. At the foot of the mountain, an elderly Plains Apache man waits in a car with his daughter while his son and a botanist from the University of Oklahoma make their way to the top. They move slowly, watching out for rattlesnakes and stepping carefully to avoid the sharp spines of prickly pear cactus and yucca. The Apache man is now too old to climb the mountain, but he is pleased to be here. He remembers how, in the past, he would come here with other Plains Apache, and how his elders would say, "Run! Run up there to the top! Get the cedars from the very top! They are the best!"

Botanists call these junipers *Juniperus pinchotii*, the redberry juniper. The Plains Apache call them *gɣad* in their language, or "mountain cedar" in English. The identification in 2007 of these junipers as *J. pinchotii* removed one of the loose ends left from the research I did in 1963 and 1964. Every researcher experiences a feeling of satisfaction when a gap in his or her data is finally filled, and I was both satisfied and exhilarated when these "mountain cedars," so important in Plains Apache culture, were finally positively identified as to species.

For generations the Plains Apache have valued the dried, fragrant leaves of mountain cedar for ceremonial and medicinal use. Yet their present knowledge of this plant is but a miniscule part of what was once an extensive body of traditional knowledge and beliefs about the

3

plant world. This body of Plains Apache traditional plant knowledge is
the subject of this ethnobotany.

THE PLAINS APACHE

Before proceeding further, let me attempt to identify clearly the ethnic
group that is the subject of this ethnobotany. The Plains Apache, as the
term is used in this book, are the Plains Indian people known to ethnographers and historians as the Kiowa Apache. I use the term "Plains Apache"
here out of respect for the wishes of tribal members, living and dead, who
never liked the label "Kiowa Apache," seldom used it, and did not wish
to be identified as part of the Kiowa tribe. (The Kiowa are a completely
separate people and speak an unrelated language.) The Plains Apache call
themselves the Apache Tribe of Oklahoma in their 1972 Constitution.
In talking to local people, they refer to themselves simply as Apache. In
talking to outsiders, they now often use the term "Plains Apache," which
sets them apart from the various Apache groups of the Southwest, as well
as from the Fort Sill Apache Tribe of Oklahoma, whose cultural and linguistic affinities are with the Chiricahua Apache of the Southwest.

The Plains Apache formerly ranged widely over the Great Plains, but
in 1867 they were assigned to a reservation in what is now southwestern
Oklahoma, which they shared with the Kiowa and the Comanche. Most
Plains Apache people today live in towns and rural communities in Caddo
and Kiowa Counties in Oklahoma. Their tribal administrative offices are
located in Anadarko, Oklahoma. A broader discussion of Plains Apache
history and traditional culture is given in chapter 1. The important point
here is that I use the term "Plains Apache" instead of the term "Kiowa
Apache" to refer to this particular group.

The Plains Apache were a typical nomadic Plains tribe, reportedly
relying heavily upon the bison for food, living in bison skin tipis, and
utilizing the hides and other parts of the bison for many items of material
culture. The early explorers and later ethnographers who described Plains
Indian culture were not knowledgeable about plants and were not interested in identifying plants of cultural significance or in describing the
extent to which wild plants were important in the culture. Yet the natural
environment of the Great Plains included a rich native flora, many species

of which could be used for food, medicines, items of material culture, and personal adornment. All of the American Indian groups that resided and traveled about on the Plains were intimately acquainted with the various microenvironments of the region. They knew how to find, harvest, and preserve the plants that were important to them. This knowledge no doubt helped ensure their survival, especially when bison were scarce. This ethnobotany hopefully contributes more information on the depth of knowledge of wild plants and their uses, not only among the Plains Apache but, by extension, among other formerly nomadic Plains groups as well.

This work is based on fieldwork done with six Plains Apache elders in 1963 and 1964. All of the elders recalled many plants that they themselves had used or that their parents, grandparents, or other older relatives had used. Thus, the information presented here should exemplify the patterns of Plains Apache plant usage from approximately 1890 to 1950. Some patterns may, in fact, be much older. Indeed, the sections on unidentified food and medicinal plants suggest that there were many other plants known and used by the Plains Apache in earlier times. However, we are fortunate that the elders of this study recalled so much and that they were willing to allow their knowledge to be written down for the benefit of future generations.

THE FIELDWORK

Most of the research for this project was conducted during the University of Oklahoma Field Schools in Ethnology and Linguistics, based in Anadarko, Oklahoma, in the summers of 1963 and 1964. My focus was on ethnobotany, and for me the eight-week period of concentrated research in June and July of each summer was divided between making field trips to collect plant specimens and interviewing elders. Usually Dr. Bittle and I spent two days each week visiting various parts of southern Caddo County and adjacent portions of Kiowa and Comanche Counties, usually in the company of an elder. At first we gathered plant specimens more or less at random and then, during the interview sessions, showed them to each elder in turn. The elders recognized many of these early specimens as significant, whereas they identified others as "just weeds," or "some kind of grass," or "a pretty flower." But as work proceeded and the elders began to realize what we wanted, they suggested trips to specific localities to collect particular plants. On these field trips we often encountered other useful plants, and elders would recall additional information concerning our plant collection. Some of the elders became genuinely interested in the study and seemed eager to contribute as much information as possible. Occasionally, an elder reported for work in the morning carrying a wilted specimen of a useful plant that he or she had come across the evening before. And there was a bit of good-natured rivalry between some elders to see who possessed the greatest store of knowledge about certain plants.

By the end of the first fieldwork season, 173 specimens, most of them representing culturally significant plants, had been collected from various localities, including mountains, rocky hills, creek bottoms, upland woods, pastures, and open prairies. A few other plants were collected in 1964, bringing the total number of specimens up to 196. Not all of the plants collected were found to be of significance in Plains Apache culture. Some specimens were duplicates of plants previously collected, and others were said by the elders to be "just weeds." Some specimen plants, such as bull nettle, poison ivy, sandbur, and goathead stickers, were known by the Apache to be noxious and unpleasant, and no use was known for them. Particularly confusing were specimens with small yellow flowers in the sunflower family, which the botanists, as well as the Apache elders, could not always identify with certainty. The total number of plants and fungi described in the chapters in part 2 and listed in table 2 in the appendix is 112 species, with several of the plants identified only to genera.

All of the plant specimens collected were numbered, labeled, and pressed. Some were identified at the field station in Anadarko, but the majority were brought back to the university at Norman and identified later by Dr. George J. Goodman, a plant systematist who was then curator of the Robert Bebb Herbarium of the University of Oklahoma. Because Dr. Goodman was an acknowledged expert on the flora of Oklahoma (Goodman 1958), his identifications may, with confidence, be considered accurate. The dried, pressed specimens of useful plants were properly mounted and deposited in the herbarium. As voucher specimens, with the name of the collector specified as W. E. Bittle, they serve as a reference for the identification of most of the plants discussed in this study.

Dr. Wayne Elisens, professor of botany and current curator of the herbarium, confirmed the identifications of nineteen of the voucher specimens in 2006. He later updated the plant nomenclature, including common names, to follow the terminology now used in the PLANTS Database (USDA, NRCS 2008). Here the updated terms are cross-referenced to older terms in both the text and the index. Several species were identified only to the genus level, and some plant identifications were made without plant specimens but based on detailed descriptions provided by the elders.

Aside from plant collecting, I spent the remainder of the five-day work week interviewing elders concerning the utilization and significance of native plants. The interviews were conducted in English, which all of the elders spoke well enough for effective communication. Each elder in turn was shown each specimen and asked to identify it and describe its significance in Apache culture. Although the interviews were kept flexible and unstructured, an attempt was made to obtain for each specimen the locally used common name, the Apache name, the meaning of the Apache name, the use of the plant in Apache culture, and any special attitudes or beliefs that might be associated with the plant. The elders were also encouraged to describe their personal experience with the plant, including where and how they gathered it. Very often during interview sessions elders would think of other plants, utilized in similar ways, or gathered at the same time of year, and would suggest where specimens of these plants might be collected on later field trips. It was found that the elders were far more successful in recognizing useful plants in the field than in interview sessions, and certainly they were more successful in identifying freshly gathered plants than dried, pressed ones. Therefore, an attempt was made to show them freshly collected plants that had not lost their characteristic odor or color.

The elders provided some of the best data when they related information concerning a particular event, such as, for example, the time they helped a relative dry a certain quantity of plums that were later eaten by rats; or when they were tricked by a cousin into smelling "sneezing medicine" on the pretense that it was "Indian perfume"; or the way the family healed an elder's sister when she had a miscarriage. Such stories were often full of valuable detail on how the plant was prepared and used in a discrete situation. The elders also quite readily admitted their ignorance of plants they did not recognize. They did not invent uses, although they could be quite inventive in providing descriptive names for unknown plants. Very often their comments about plants they did not recognize were phrased like this: "I don't know that plant. Maybe somebody else might use it and know it, but me, I don't know it. Just the ones I use and my mother [or other relative] use, I know them."

Field notes were taken in a longhand form as near to verbatim as possible, so that every shred of information would be preserved in the elder's own phraseology and word choice. The notes were typed up in duplicate and indexed according to conventional ethnographic categories immediately following each interview. Copies of these field notes are now in the possession of the author and will eventually be deposited in the Western History Division of the University of Oklahoma Library.

THE PLAINS APACHE ELDERS

Data for this work were obtained by interviewing six Plains Apache elders intensively and collecting specimens of significant plants for botanical identification. The six elders were Ray Blackbear, Connie May (Datose) Saddleblanket, Fred Bigman, Louise (Susagossa) Saddleblanket, Rose Chaletsin, and Gertrude Chalepah. All of the elders except Gertrude were recruited by Dr. William E. Bittle, with the help of Ray Blackbear, with whom he had worked previously on a study of the Plains Apache language. I became acquainted with Gertrude through my work with her mother, Rose Chaletsin, which led me to meet other members of her family. I soon learned that although Gertrude was the youngest of the elders, she possessed a great deal of knowledge about Apache medicines and plant use. She contributed greatly to my understanding of Apache medicines and doctoring practices.

I and the other field school students quickly became comfortable talking with the elders, and some of us developed quite close and, in some cases, lifelong friendships with them and members of their families. (This is one of the several reasons I use their first names in this book.) We found the Plains Apache people generally to be welcoming and hospitable. Once convinced that we had a serious and respectful interest in their history and culture, they seemed pleased. They invited us to social gatherings, such as song practice sessions, bingo games, church services, and dances. Part of the reason for their positive attitude toward us, I believe, was the fact that they had had satisfying experiences with anthropologists in the past, anthropologists such as James Mooney, J. Gilbert McAllister, Charles S. Brant, and, of course, William E. Bittle.

Much of our interaction with the elders and other Plains Apache people was interlaced with humor and laughter. The Plains Apache value a keen sense of humor. They joke, laugh, and tease one another a great deal when they get together. We field school students provided endless entertainment for them as we tried to pronounce Apache words, slice meat properly, make palatable fry bread (a near-universal modern "Indian" food), erect a brush arbor, or learn Apache dance steps. Sometimes Plains Apache friends resorted to subterfuge to help a student out of a difficult situation.

One young female field school student developed a close friendship with an older Plains Apache woman who was noted for the quality of her fry bread. The student had been selected by her peers to make fry bread for the rest of the students while they were camping with the Apache at the summer Blackfeet Dance gathering. This student did not know how to cook anything, let alone fry bread, and she confided her fears to her Apache friend. The next morning, before dawn, the student became aware that someone was pulling up the bottom edge of the tipi near her cot. "Here's your fry bread!" the Apache woman whispered as she pushed a large bowl of dough into the tipi. A little later the other students were amazed when they were presented with tasty, golden-brown fry bread to eat with their black boiled coffee for breakfast, while, from a distance, several Apache women looked on with great amusement. This incident was the cause of many jokes and much laughter for the rest of the summer as the student was teased about her expertise in making fry bread.

Brief biographies and comments about the six Apache elders are given below.

Ray Blackbear

Ray was born in 1903 in the Hatchetville community and lived all his life there and in nearby Boone. His parents, Joe and Priscilla Blackbear, were both traditionalists with strong nostalgia for the former way of life. However, from about 1911 he was raised by his paternal grandparents, who spoke very little English. He learned a great deal about traditional Plains Apache culture from these elders, especially his grandfather, Old Man Blackbear, who for years told him endless stories embodying the history and folklore of the Apache. Ray heard these stories, told in wintertime, over and over again, gaining mastery over the many intricate details. His grandfather also taught him much about finding and using native plants, such as when and where to gather wild plums, grapes, or mulberries and how to select materials for making bows and arrows.

Ray completed the ninth grade at the Boone Public School and had one year of vocational training at Haskell Institute in Kansas. He loved to read, and he developed a lifelong commitment to studying Apache history and traditional way of life. Beginning in 1953 he worked several years with Dr. Bittle on a study of the grammar of the Kiowa Apache language (Bittle 1956, 1963). This long association with an anthropologist gave him an exceptional ability to grasp the goals of our ethnobotanical research.

Ray and his wife, Helen, a Kiowa, were always exceedingly kind to me, although Ray used to tease me unmercifully about my inability to pronounce the Apache term, *sǫ ch'ił* (blackjack oak), correctly. Twist my tongue as I might in every conceivable position, I could never get the term properly, and he would laugh uproariously at my efforts. Ray and Helen often invited me and other students to their home near the Boone community for a meal and to spend the night. They were proud of their two-story frame home, which had been built by the federal government for Old Man Blackbear in the early twentieth century. The house, unadorned by trees or bushes, was situated on high ground on a native prairie, overlooking the timber-fringed course of Tahoe Creek. For years Ray used to haul drinking water in five-gallon containers from a well at the Apache Baptist Church, several miles away, as the water-well drilling technology of the time could not reach potable underground water under his land. Despite this inconvenience, Ray and Helen did not want to move. They loved this place on the prairie for its natural beauty, tranquility, and connection to family and Apache history.

Ray Blackbear was an active participant in peyote ceremonies, and he had a rich, beautiful singing voice. He knew many old songs of the Manatidie, a men's dancing society, and he composed several new ones.

Ray died in 1967.

Helen and Ray Blackbear, 1963.

Connie May (Datose) Saddleblanket

Connie May Saddleblanket, born in 1888, and Fred Bigman, born in 1900, were sister and brother. Connie May was born in a tipi in an Apache encampment north of Anadarko. Both were raised by their traditionally minded parents, who did not speak English, and they learned early to speak the Apache language with fluency. Both parents possessed and used family medicines containing plant ingredients, and both were knowledgeable in the collection and preparation of edible plants.

Connie May remembered many details of life during the reservation period, which ended in 1901, when the Apache were made to take 160-acre allotments in severalty. She learned from her older relatives much about wild plant foods and medicines prepared from plants, and she listened to many stories told by her parents and grandparents about life in former times. She attended the Methvin Mission School in Anadarko for a few months in 1901 but was removed from the school when her mother became ill with smallpox and needed assistance at home. She never returned to school, although eventually she did learn English. She continued to live with her parents, where she helped care for her baby brother and did other camp chores, until she was about fifteen, when she married Homer Saddleblanket. Considerably older than Connie May, Homer was the adopted son of Saddleblanket, a noted Plains Apache doctor and peyote leader. Homer was the half-brother of Louise Saddleblanket, who was thus Connie May's sister-in-law. The two women maintained a close relationship throughout their lives.

At the time of our study, Connie May, the oldest of the elders we interviewed, was a slender woman, still physically active and very much in control of her life. Her English was somewhat harder to understand than that of the other elders, for she had had less formal schooling and fewer interactions with English-speaking persons when she was young. I learned to listen carefully to her answers to my questions, so that I soon adjusted to her accent and style of expression. I also learned to speak slowly and distinctly in addressing her, using common English words and avoiding complex words and constructions. I would wait patiently while she formulated her responses, which often were rich and detailed descriptions of Plains Apache life in the late nineteenth and early twentieth centuries. Embedded in these descriptions were many of her personal experiences with wild plant foods, medicines, and doctoring practices. She said many times that she wanted to tell me only what she knew—what she had seen, heard, or done. She was reluctant to recount hearsay information, afraid she might get something wrong.

I visited Connie May several times after the fieldwork was done. She and her granddaughter always welcomed me with coffee and conversation, and we enjoyed reminiscing about the field schools and our study of Plains Apache plant usage.

Connie May died in 1968.

Louise Saddleblanket (Susagossa) and Connie May Saddleblanket (Datose), July 1961.

Fred Bigman

Fred Bigman, Connie May's younger brother, lived most of his life in the area around Fort Cobb and Carnegie, Oklahoma. His father and some other relatives had allotments on the south side of the Washita River. His father, Bigman, was one of the few Plains Apache who made a serious attempt to farm, raising primarily corn and kaffir corn, a grain sorghum, on about forty-five acres of bottomland. Fred assisted his father with farm work, and when his father grew old, he took over management of the farm duties. He gave up farming in 1925 but did sporadic farm labor for others for many years. He married Annie Somti, a Kiowa, in 1920.

Fred was devoted to his mother and father and listened attentively to their stories and advice. During the field schools he provided useful information on edible plants and plant medicines. In addition, he was of great help in clarifying the meanings of many Apache names for plants and plant parts. He was a peyote leader, and he loved to talk about the Native American Church and the paraphernalia used in peyote meetings.

I found Fred to be sociable and easy to talk to. He seemed to be quite interested in the field school students and their activities. He lived very close to the rented bungalow that was our field station in Anadarko in 1963, and he would walk to the house, usually arriving around seven o'clock in the morning even though our interviews were supposed to begin at eight o'clock. Sometimes his wife, Annie, would come with him. She was fascinated by the dormitory-like sleeping arrangements for the female students on the back sleeping porch, and she would station her chair so as to observe everything going on there. Fred would sit quietly in the kitchen, smoking a cigarette, drinking a cup of coffee, and making small talk with anyone willing to converse at that hour of the morning. Sometimes we got the distinct impression that watching the field school students wake up was their favorite form of entertainment!

I continued to visit Fred and Annie Bigman for several years after my fieldwork was completed. They were kind and gentle people, holding on to traditional ways as best they could in a changing world.

Fred died in the early seventies.

Louise (Susagossa) Saddleblanket

Louise Saddleblanket was born in 1893 and lived most of her life around the communities of Carnegie, Apache, and Boone. Her father, Saddle-blanket, was considerably older than her mother, and he had participated in hunting and raiding expeditions before the Plains Apache were forced into reservation life in 1869. Through a vision quest and prayer he became a noted doctor whose powers were greatly respected and also feared. He was also one of the first Plains Apache peyote leaders. Louise was his only child (although he adopted her half-brother, Homer), and he lavished attention and favors on her. Although she preferred the company of her father, she learned much about traditional Apache women's work from her

Fred Bigman, 1967.

mother, including gathering wild plant foods and firewood, tanning hides, sewing, and beadwork. Louise attended the Cache Creek Presbyterian Mission School, west of Apache, Oklahoma, and the Methvin Mission School and St. Patrick's Mission School, both located in Anadarko, completing seven or eight grades. She spoke English well. At age eighteen she married Hiram Hummingbird, a Kiowa, and they lived for many years in Carnegie, close to his relatives. Later she married Frank Charcoal, an Arapaho, and last she married Emmet Tsotigh, a Kiowa.

One of the Apache elders we interviewed thought that Louise had lived so long among the Kiowa that she sometimes confused Apache and Kiowa traditions. However, I found Louise to have excellent recall of things told her by her Apache parents and other relatives, and she was especially good at remembering Apache plant names. From my close association with Louise I learned something of the economic challenges facing many Plains Apache, including the hardships they face in getting to town, to stores, to medical facilities, and even to local Indian community social events. Yet Louise, despite her financial problems, exhibited an innate dignity in her interactions with the field school personnel. She took pride in her identity as an Apache woman and as daughter of a respected Apache medicine man.

Louise also had the ability to laugh at herself and others. She would sometimes mimic in a comical way the movements of men doing the Manatidie Dance. She also had a salacious streak, which she sometimes employed when we were well beyond the hearing of the male Apache elders.

Louise was one of the elders who remembered some of the old-time Manatidie Dance songs, and she assisted in the 1958 revival of the dance. She also showed considerable enthusiasm for the ethnobotanical research, accompanying me and Dr. Bittle a number of times on area field trips in search of culturally significant plants. Since the other elders all acknowledged that Louise was good at piercing ears, I asked her if she would pierce mine. She did so, using a carefully selected, long thorn of a prickly pear cactus (*Opuntia macrorhiza*). She did a good job, and I always think of her when I wear earrings for pierced ears.

Louise died in 1976.

Rose Chaletsin

Rose Chaletsin was born in a tipi in 1893. Her grandparents died when she was a small child, and she was raised by her parents and other relatives in various encampments around Anadarko. After allotment in 1901, her family moved to the Boone vicinity, where they lived in a tent on one of the family allotments. She attended a mission school for three years. At age fifteen she married Alonzo Chalepah, an older man who was active in tribal dances and also well respected for his medicine powers. They had several children, one of whom, Gertrude Chalepah, was an elder interviewed for this study. In 1928 Rose left Alonzo and married Apache Ben Chaletsin. Apache Ben, who had been born in 1867, had experienced late-nineteenth century Plains Apache culture, and he was a great storyteller. He was a peyote leader and a charter member of the Native American Church, founded in 1918.

Both of Rose's husbands were prominent and influential figures among the Plains Apache, and no doubt Rose's own extensive knowledge of traditional Apache culture was greatly expanded by listening to their reminiscences of life before her time, and listening as well to their telling of Apache stories. Rose herself was an accomplished storyteller, punctuating her recitations with hand slaps and vocal sound effects. Although the Apache usually told their stories in wintertime, she consented to allow some of us to tape record a few of her stories during the field schools. We did so one evening at her home, using a now-vintage Wollensak reel-to-reel recorder. I was fortunate enough to be present at the recording session, and I remember how she laughed heartily when the tape was played back.

Rose was a woman of property and a dominant figure in her large extended family. She was strong-willed and usually arranged events to her satisfaction, sometimes without saying a word. For example, she became very fond of a female graduate student in the 1961 field school. She and the student soon developed a grandmother-granddaughter relationship, one that is very close in Plains Apache culture. That summer the student accompanied Rose and her family to the Mescalero Apache Reservation in New Mexico, where they attended the annual Fourth of

July Girl's Puberty Ceremony and accompanying tribal dances. At that time the Mescalero did not want non-Indians to attend parts of their celebration. The student received hostile, unfriendly looks and felt distinctly unwelcome. That first night, when the evening dances began, Rose said to the student, "I want you to carry my folding chair and take my arm and walk with me out to where the women are singing." The student did as she was told. She helped Rose find a place for her chair and helped arrange her shawl. After that, the Mescalero treated the student with the same friendliness and hospitality they extended to the visiting Plains Apache.

I enjoyed working with Rose and listening to some of her insightful opinions about Apache life in former times. (One time she commented that in the old days the women did all the work and the men did nothing but sit around on horseback.) At the time of our research, Rose was blind, but she could identify many plant specimens by touch and by smell. Sometimes we had to give her a clue, suggesting the common name of the plant or providing an Apache name we had learned from another elder. She could often provide a rich detail of information on the use of those plants she knew or remembered.

Rose Chaletsin died in 1965.

Gertrude Chalepah

Gertrude Chalepah, daughter of Rose and Alonzo Chalepah, was born in 1914. She was the youngest of the six elders we interviewed. Because of a dislocated hip that never healed correctly, she had never gone to school. She was raised by traditionally minded grandparents and was an astute observer of their practices, as well as an avid listener to their stories. She understood and spoke the Apache language well. She possessed knowledge of native plants and medicines gained from paying careful attention to what her elders did and said, and she had an excellent memory. She lived all her life in close proximity to her large extended family. She was skilled in sewing and in the traditional women's crafts of beadwork and working with hides. Over the years she made many pairs of moccasins and dance costume items for members of her family. Devoted to the old ways, she was a firm believer in the traditional

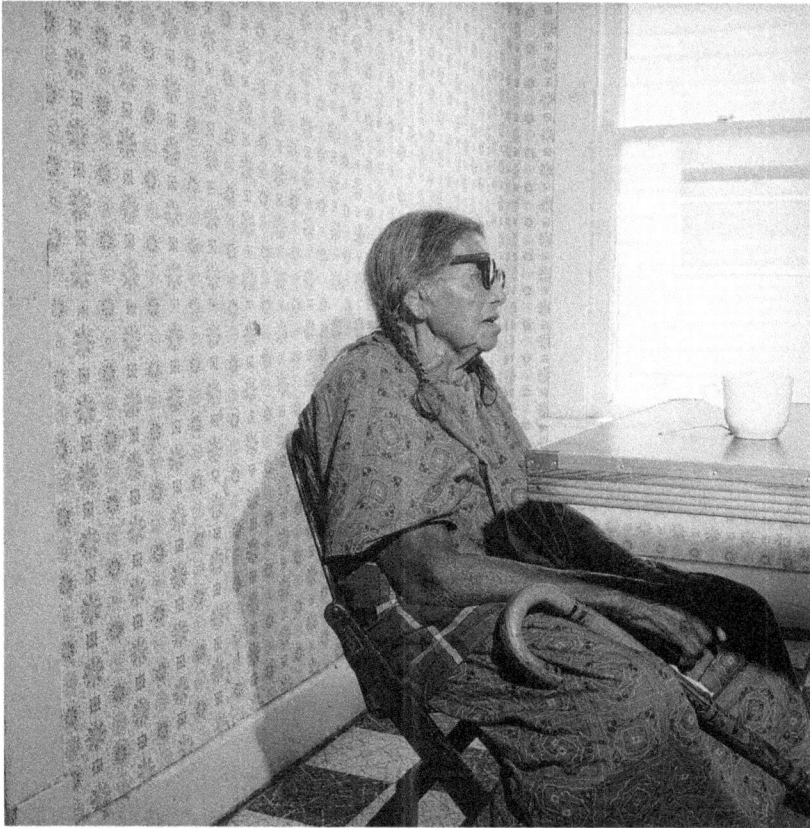

Rose Chaletsin, 1963.

methods of doctoring and healing, including the effectiveness of Apache plant medicines. As older members of her extended family died, she became the inheritor and caretaker of surviving family medicines, some of which are described in this book.

I first met Gertrude in the summer of 1963, when all of the field school participants were invited to watch the Chalepah family butcher and process a young beef steer. The meat was to be cut into portions and divided up among the camps at the summer Apache Manatidie Dance gathering. Gertrude and other women of the family stood in the shade of a tree, sharpening their well-used butcher knives, while the men killed the animal, skinned it, cut off the head, and cut the carcass into quarters.

Gertrude Chalepah, 1965.

Then the women went to work, cutting up the meat into family portions. They salvaged the heart, liver, and other edible internal organs, and they carefully cleaned and rinsed the small intestine, which they would later prepare for frying or making into "Indian sausage." They offered us samples of the raw liver and the bone marrow, which they called "Indian butter." Later Gertrude made Indian sausage for us by filling a section of the small intestine with chunks of beef tenderloin and onion and tying off the ends. The sausage was then grilled over a bed of coals. It was delicious.

Gertrude and I developed a close friendship that ended only with her death. She accompanied me on trips to the peyote fields in south Texas, to Zuni Pueblo in New Mexico, and to the Mescalero Apache reservation

Julia Jordan in the field, 1963. From the author's collection.

in New Mexico. She was a quiet, soft-spoken, and serious person who devoted her life to the service of her extended family and the preservation of her family's traditional Apache knowledge.

Gertrude Chalepah died in 1984.

DATA PRESENTATION

The rest of this book is a presentation of data on the Plains Apache and their knowledge of the plant world. Chapter 1 presents information on Plains Apache history and traditional culture in order to show that these people were gatherers of wild plants and hunters of bison and other game on the Great Plains for at least several hundred years. Chapter 2 deals with their conceptualization of the plant world, including the relation of people to nature, native Apache plant categories, and the concept of plants existing in pairs.

Chapters 3 through 6 in part 2 of this book list the wild plants identified through this fieldwork as being of cultural significance in Plains Apache culture and provide detailed descriptions of the cultural contexts in which the plants were used. I am sure that many other wild plants were formerly used, but knowledge of their identity and use is probably beyond recovery. Tables 1 and 2 in the conclusion summarize information on the plants and fungi of use to the Plains Apache.

Since my main fieldwork ended, in 1965, botanists have revised the system of scientific plant names and have rearranged the grouping and naming of some plants. Therefore, I have cross-referenced the older terms in the text and in the index. The older terms are enclosed in parentheses and preceded by an equals sign. The full scientific plant names, including authorities, are given when the plants are first named at the beginning of individual plant sections. The full scientific names are also given in table 2, which is a listing of all the useful plants in this study. The scientific names used within the body of the text denote genus and species only.

Part 1

The Plains Apache

An ethnobotany is a study of the interrelationships between people and plants. To understand the use of plants by a particular people, one must know something of their history, their culture, and the natural environments in which they have lived.

Part 1 of this ethnobotany introduces the Plains Apache as an American Indian people who lived on the Great Plains for hundreds of years and are now residents of Oklahoma. Their known history and nineteenth-century culture are reviewed briefly as a background for understanding their knowledge and use of native plants. The geographical setting is described, and the Plains Apache view of the plant world is explored.

Chapter 1

Plains Apache History and Culture

EARLY HISTORY

Among the historic nomadic Plains Indian tribes whose nineteenth-century way of life—replete with horses, travois, bison hunts, tipis, war bonnets, medicine bundles, and raiding parties—is so well known, the Plains Apache may well lay claim to having resided on the Plains longer than any of the others. They are, in all probability, descended from one or more of the Apachean groups that were living on the high plains at the time of the Coronado Expedition in 1541.

The Plains Apache have been known to historians and ethnographers by various names, including "Gattacka" or "Kataka," "Kaskaia," "Prairie Apache," and "Kiowa Apache." This last name was applied to them in the late nineteenth century because they were usually associated with the Kiowa in their dealings with the United States. In their own language they called themselves Nadiisha-déna (Mooney 1898: 245), of which *déna* means "people." Informally, tribal members refer to themselves as "Apache," and they increasingly use the term "Plains Apache" when they need to distinguish themselves from the Fort Sill Apache Tribe of Oklahoma. (The latter are descendants of those members of Geronimo's band of Chiricahua Apache who chose to settle in Oklahoma in 1913 following imprisonment in Florida and Alabama from 1886 to 1894 and later at Fort Sill, Oklahoma, from 1894 to 1913 [Opler 1983: 408–409].) Throughout this book I refer to the people who are the subject of this ethnobotany and their known antecedents as "Plains Apache," or, simply, "Apache." Groups speaking related languages but whose specific tribal designations are unknown will be referred to as "Apacheans."

The Plains Apache language belongs to the Apachean branch of the Athabaskan language family. This family is widely distributed in western North America, with a northern group located throughout much of western Canada and Alaska, a Pacific coastal group located in northern California and British Columbia, and a southern group, the Apacheans, located on the plains and in the southwest of the United States. Other languages in the Apachean branch are Navajo, San Carlos, Chiricahua, Mescalero, Lipan, and Jicarilla. The Plains Apache language differs more from these six than they differ among themselves, indicating early separation of the Plains Apache from speakers of the other Apachean languages.

The Apacheans probably migrated southward from Canada along the high plains corridor just east of the foothills of the Rocky Mountains. It has been suggested (D. Gunnerson 1956: 361; 1974: 127–28) that in the north they may have been hunters of large herd animals, the barren ground variety of caribou. Therefore they could have adapted fairly quickly to the hunting of bison, also large herd animals, as they moved south onto the plains. They came over a period of time, as bands or groups of related extended families, not as a single, cohesive group or migration. There were probably dialectical differences even before the general movement southward took place (Hoijer 1971: 5).

At the time of first contact by Europeans, there were a number of Apachean-speaking groups living on the plains. All were nomadic people living primarily on the bison but also hunting deer, antelope, and various small game animals. They also gathered wild plant foods and traded with settled Puebloan peoples, exchanging meat, tallow, hides, and salt for corn and other produce. The Coronado Expedition of 1541 encountered two Apachean groups, whom they called "Querecho" and "Teya," respectively. A chronicler of the expedition described the way of life of the Querecho as follows:

> These Indians live or sustain themselves entirely from the cattle, for they neither grow nor harvest maize. With the skins they build their houses; with the skins they clothe and shoe themselves; from the skins they make ropes and also obtain wool. With the sinews they make thread, with which they sew their clothes and also their tents.

From the bones they shape awls. The dung they use for firewood, since there is no other fuel in that land. The bladders they use as jugs and drinking containers. They sustain themselves on their meat, eating it slightly roasted and heated over the dung. . . .

These people have dogs similar to those of Spain, except that they are somewhat larger. They load these dogs like beasts of burden and make light pack-saddles for them, cinching them with leather straps. . . . When these Indians move—for they have no permanent residence anywhere, since they follow the cattle to find food—these dogs carry their homes for them. In addition to what they carry on their backs, they carry poles for the tents, dragging them fastened to their saddles . . . (quoted in Wedel 1961: 304).

The Spaniards were amazed at the great herds of bison and equally amazed at the extent to which the "Querecho" depended on them. The nature of the contact precluded any mention of plants in this chronicle. However, the pack saddles and tent poles mentioned undoubtedly came from plant materials.

Waldo R. Wedel (1961: 289), using the term "Plains Apaches" in a generic sense, has suggested that "The Plains Apaches, as full-fledged pedestrian bison-hunters whom the Spanish called the *Querecho*, were certainly in the southern High Plains shortly after 1500; before that, they were quite likely in the plains north of the Arkansas, but no convincing archaeological evidence of their passage has yet come to light here."

Some Plains Apacheans, accustomed to trading with Taos Pueblo, may have acquired a few horses by 1659 (Swagerty 2001: 260), but the real opportunity to procure horses came during the Pueblo Revolt of 1680–82, when the Pueblos obtained thousands of Spanish horses, most of which were transferred to Plains Indian groups through trade or theft (Haines 1938a: 117). The Plains Apache, and probably also the Kiowa, were among the groups that acquired the horse early. In 1682, the French explorer La Salle heard that there were tribes called the "Gattacka" and the "Manhroet" living south of the Pawnee villages, and that they lived upon the great herds of bison and had large herds of horses, which he believed they had stolen from the Spanish settlements in the Southwest (Mooney

1898: 248; Foster and McCollough 2001: 927). There is little doubt that the "Gattacka" were the historical Plains Apache, who were known later to representatives of the United States as "Kataka" or "Catarka." The "Manhroet" may have been the Kiowa. Both tribes became instrumental in spreading the horse to other tribes, first to those village groups with whom they were already trading and later to other nomadic peoples such as the Arapaho and Cheyenne.

Lewis and Clark reported in 1805 that the Plains Apache (whom they called the "Cataka") were living in the Black Hills region of northeastern Wyoming, with the Kiowa near them. Both tribes were rich in horses, which they were trading to the Arikara and Mandan villages of the upper Missouri River region (Mooney 1898: 251). The French trader Antoine Tabeau, who lived with the Arikara in 1803–1804, wrote that the "Catarkas" were at the foot of the Black Hills with several other tribes, including the "Chayenne" and the "Caninanbiches" [Arapaho] (Abel 1939: 98, 154). The Cheyenne had only recently arrived on the plains, and the Sioux were still residing near the Missouri River. The Comanche had established themselves on the southern plains by the 1730s, displacing most Apachean groups to the south and southwest (Kavanaugh 2001: 886). Presumably, the Plains Apache and the Kiowa had for some time been participating in the intertribal trade centering in the Black Hills in which horses from the Spanish Southwest were exchanged for guns coming into the area from the northeast. They obtained most of their horses from the Spanish settlements and traded them to the northern tribes.

The period of residence in the Black Hills region was apparently memorable in the history of both the Plains Apache and the Kiowa. Both are linked by their oldest traditions to this area, and their most sacred medicines are said to have originated there. Possibly also at this time of peaceful and intensive interaction with the northern tribes they adopted such traits as warrior societies and medicine bundles.

After 1805 the Cheyenne and Arapaho gradually moved to their historic location on the central plains at the base of the Rocky Mountains, while the Plains Apache and the Kiowa were found increasingly to the south. The latter tribes ranged widely over the high plains from the Red River to the Platte, but eventually they came to regard the country south of the Arkansas River as their home range (Jablow 1950: 65). Although no important trading post was located in their territory, they obtained guns and other manufactured goods at either Bent's Fort, on the Arkansas, or its smaller branch, Fort Adobe, on the South Canadian, and through trade with New Mexican settlements.

The Plains Apache usually maintained peaceful relations with their neighbors on the southern and central plains. When hostilities flared between the Kiowa and Cheyenne in the 1830s, the Plains Apache remained neutral and finally assisted the Arapaho in bringing about a peace agreement in 1840 (Jablow 1950: 72–75). From that time on the Arapaho, Cheyenne, Plains Apache, Kiowa, and Comanche were generally friendly toward each other and hostile to such tribes as the Ute, Navajo, Pawnee, and Osage.

Because of the unsettled conditions prevailing in the eighteenth and nineteenth centuries, the small Plains Apache tribe tended to associate itself with a larger, more powerful group, usually the Kiowa. The relationship was one of mutual advantage in matters of trade and defense, and the Plains Apache maintained their independence from other tribes. They occasionally left the Kiowa and camped with the Arapaho or Cheyenne, and during the few interludes of comparative peace on the plains, they sometimes camped completely apart from other tribes.

NINETEENTH-CENTURY PLAINS CULTURE

Despite language and several other characteristics linking them to other Apacheans, most of whom by 1750 were in the Southwest, the Plains Apache way of life was basically similar to that of other nomadic, horse-using tribes of the plains. The economy was based upon hunting the bison, which furnished not only food but raw materials for making lodge covers, clothing, and many other necessary articles. Bison meat was by far the preferred food, although deer, antelope, elk, and other animals were also eaten. Fresh meat was prepared by roasting or boiling, and surplus meat was sliced thin, dried in the sun, and thus preserved for later use. Pemmican was made from dried meat pounded with tallow and fruit such as choke cherries or plums. Wild plant foods, especially

in the form of edible roots, nuts, and fruits, were also important con-
stituents of the diet. Maize, tobacco, and other horticultural produce
were sometimes obtained by trade with farming groups, an example
being the exchange between the Arikara, who were farmers, and eight
plains nomadic groups at the foot of the Black Hills, noted by Tabeau in
1804 (Abel 1939: 154).

The hunting was done by men, who went out in small groups throughout most of the year, usually on horseback. Tribal hunts were held in the
summer after the Kiowa Sun Dance, and also late in the fall. These communal hunts were strictly policed by the Manatidie, or Blackfeet Society,
the largest men's warrior society. Individuals who disobeyed tribal rules
about the hunt were punished by being whipped and having some horses
killed and perhaps their tipi or other property destroyed.

Almost every man became a warrior and was expected to fight if
the camp was attacked, as well as to demonstrate his manhood by going
on war journeys into enemy country. Most of these expeditions were
composed of a small number of men going after horses and other plunder.
Some, however, set out for the purpose of taking scalps or killing the
enemy, often in retaliation for some previous injury. Boys were trained
from childhood in the use of weapons and taught to be brave and to
endure hardships without complaining. The most respected men in the
tribe were those with good war records who had accumulated large horse
herds through their raiding activities.

Most of the routine activities of camp life were carried on within
the extended family. Such a group consisted of several related nuclear
families, each with its own tipi, who camped close to each other. Women
often cooperated in such tasks as slicing meat, dressing hides, and
gathering wild plant foods. Young men tended the horses together and
hunted, while older men often assisted each other in making weapons
and ceremonial equipment. The older people of both sexes also contributed importantly to the welfare of the family group. In addition to
performing many tasks around camp, they helped train their grandchildren
in adult skills and proper behavior. At night they told endless stories,
which entertained everyone and served to educate the young in the
accumulated knowledge and traditions of the Plains Apache.

The Plains Apache usually numbered around three to four hundred persons, making up a very close-knit group. Since a large number of relatives were recognized through both parents, everyone was related in some way to every other member of the tribe. However, in actual practice some of the more distant relationships were lightly regarded or ignored. The preferred form of marriage was with persons within the tribe but outside one's immediate circle of relatives. Some intertribal marriages did take place, however, including marriage with women captured from other tribes. Men who were good providers sometimes had more than one wife, usually marrying two or more sisters.

Throughout much of the year the tribe was to be found in several bands or camps, though these usually remained close to each other. Each camp had its leader, or headman, a man of maturity and proven practical knowledge who might also own one of the sacred medicine bundles. Although his advice was likely to be taken seriously, his authority was limited and the component families of his group could and often did take up residence elsewhere whenever they pleased. The whole tribe came together for such events as the Kiowa Sun Dance and the communal tribal hunts, as well as for intertribal trade gatherings and peace councils. There was no single head chief, although in later years the U.S. government recognized certain individuals as having the power to approve its policies for the tribe.

There were four societies that, like those of other Plains Indian tribes, served military, social, and ceremonial ends. Most men belonged to the Manatidie (*máánatí de'é*) society, which held an annual dance every spring and other dances throughout the year, usually before a war party set out. The Manatidie acted as a police force during tribal encampments and marches, and its members regulated the tribal hunts. The society also helped families who were in need or in mourning, bringing gifts of food and other items. Its leaders were four highly respected warriors, each of whom owned a fur-wrapped staff or ceremonial lance. These staffs were displayed at the society's dances, and certain supernatural powers were connected with them.

The Klintidie *(łį́įtí'de'é)*, or Horse Society, was smaller and composed of men with outstanding war records. Members of the organization were committed to act with extreme bravery—even recklessness—in battle. Little is known of this society, though we do know that members were supposed to engage in contrary behavior, or do things backwards. A woman's society, the Izuwe, held secret ceremonies that were supposed to benefit the whole tribe, especially warriors.

All children, both boys and girls, belonged to the Kasowe, or Rabbit Society, and participated in its dance, which was directed by the owner of the most important medicine bundle. Through this dance the children from all families came to know each other well. Together they learned the ways of society membership and their future responsibilities as adults.

Religious practices centered upon certain medicine bundles that, according to tradition, had been given to the tribe long ago through supernatural favor. There were four of these bundles in later years, each containing sacred and highly revered objects, including some medicines and other plant materials used for ritual purification. The bundles possessed the power to guard the welfare of the tribe and bestow blessings upon individuals who came and prayed to them. These bundles were inherited through the male line, and the annual ceremonies for their renewal and purification were directed at bringing health and long life to all members of the tribe. The bundle owners alone had the right to settle disputes between individuals and families. Once their decision was requested, everyone had to abide by it.

In most years the Plains Apache attended the Kiowa Sun Dance early in the summer, and they had a set place among the Kiowa bands in the large camp circle on this occasion. The ceremony was directed by the owner of the most sacred Kiowa medicine, the Taime bundle. The Manatidie society was given certain tasks to perform, and individual Plains Apache men could participate in the Kiowa dance. The Plains Apache enjoyed the excitement and festivities of the Sun Dance encampment, and they regarded the ceremony as beneficial to themselves as well as to the Kiowa. However, their own medicine bundles were of much greater importance in their religious life.

The Plains Apache made their first treaty with the United States in 1837 under the name Ka-ta-ka. The Kiowa and Tawakoni (a branch of the Wichita) were also parties to this treaty, which was signed at Fort Gibson in Indian Territory. The signing tribes agreed to maintain peaceful and friendly relations with the United States, and also with the Osage and Creek tribes. The latter were also to have the privilege of hunting bison in western Indian Territory, a provision that was probably not understood by the plains tribes.

The Plains Apache signed their next treaty at Fort Atkinson, Kansas, in 1853, along with the Kiowa and Comanche. By this time the plains tribes had begun to feel the pinch of the encroaching American frontier. Overland travel had increased rapidly after the Mexican War, and as a result, game was greatly diminished in some areas and severe epidemics of smallpox and cholera ravaged the tribes every few years. This treaty provided that the Indians would receive annuities of food, clothing, and other goods for a period of ten years. In return the tribes were to allow the government to establish roads and military posts within their territory. They were also to stop making raids into Mexico, return all Mexican captives, and cease fighting with other tribes.

After this treaty, however, the basic causes of unrest continued unabated. The promised annuities were often in short supply and erratic in reaching their destination. As game continued to decrease, the Kiowa resumed their raiding, and the Plains Apache, inclined to be peaceful, gravitated more toward the Arapaho and Cheyenne. In 1862 they were informally "adopted" into the Arapaho tribe so as to share with them and the Cheyenne the reservation in southeastern Colorado established by the Fort Wise Treaty of 1861 (Bittle: 1971). Their affiliation with the Arapaho became official in 1865, when they detached themselves from the Kiowa and joined the Cheyenne and Arapaho in signing the Treaty of the Little Arkansas. By its terms the Plains Apache were to share with these tribes a reservation located between the Arkansas and Cimarron rivers in Kansas and Indian Territory, now Oklahoma.

A number of important Indian leaders never signed the Treaty of the Little Arkansas, however, and fighting soon broke out again. The government's last effort to deal peacefully with the five southern plains tribes and induce them to accept settled life on a reservation resulted in the Treaty of Medicine Lodge, which the Plains Apache signed on October 21, 1867. At this time they severed their connection with the Cheyenne and Arapaho and rejoined the Kiowa and Comanche. The three tribes were given a reservation of almost 3 million acres lying between the Washita and Red rivers in western Indian Territory. The government would pay annuities for thirty years and furnish the Indians with seed, implements, and farming instruction. For their part, the Indians were to withdraw their opposition to the building of railroads and military posts on their land and refrain from molesting travelers and raiding in Texas and Mexico.

A number of hostilities occurred after the Medicine Lodge Treaty, and a few Plains Apache individuals stayed with the hostile factions of the Kiowa, Comanche, and Cheyenne until peace finally came in 1875. For the most part, however, the tribe remained neutral, remaining close to the agency at Fort Sill as the final wars on the southern plains were fought. Within a few years the bison were gone and the Indians had no choice but to accept reservation life and learn new ways.

THE RESERVATION AND ALLOTMENT PERIODS

The Plains Apache, like other tribes, found the new ways strange and unattractive but, with the bison gone, they realized the necessity for change and made an effort to reorient their lives. Subsistence at first came from a combination of sources, including government annuities, the hunting of deer and small game, gathering wild plant foods, and income from jobs around the agency. Eventually many Plains Apache began to raise garden produce such as corn, pumpkins, watermelons, cantaloupes, and cucumbers for their own use, and a few began to raise cattle and other livestock. As schools, churches, and trading posts were established, the Indians began to adopt many of the external trappings of American frontier life.

Nevertheless, the Plains Apache were often discouraged with their new life and looked back with nostalgia and regret at the time when they were free to travel over the plains and hunt bison as they pleased. Then in 1890, an Arapaho prophet, Sitting Bull, introduced the Ghost Dance religion to the Kiowa and Plains Apache (Mooney 1898: 359). Its basic tenet was that a new world was coming in which the white man would have no part. The bison would return, dead relatives would be restored to life, and all Indian people would live in harmony with each other. At first many Plains Apache accepted and participated in the

Ghost Dance. But as time passed and the basic promises remained unfulfilled, their enthusiasm waned. Although a few individuals continued to attend Ghost Dance gatherings until at least 1910 (Brant 1969: 17), most Plains Apache eventually turned to the peyote religion as a more satisfying form of worship.

The peyote ritual had been introduced to the Plains Apache around 1875 by a man named Nayokogał, who was either a Lipan or a Mescalero Apache (Brant 1950: 212). It involved the ceremonial eating of a spineless cactus, peyote (*Lophophora williamsii*), in a blend of native and Christian religious elements. The Plains Apache became noted for the strength of their belief in the peyote way, and they helped spread it to the Arapaho, Southern Cheyenne, and other Oklahoma tribes. After considerable opposition, the peyote religion gained legal status in 1918, when the Native American Church was established with a charter under Oklahoma state laws (La Barre 1964: 170–71). It has continued as an important form of worship to this day. Many Plains Apache also joined Christian churches, the Methodist and Baptist denominations dominating in their territory.

In the late nineteenth century, many non-Indian groups pressured the government to open the Indian lands. The Kiowa-Apache-Comanche reservation was finally abolished in 1901. All members of the three tribes received individual allotments of 160 acres, with the Plains Apache receiving 150 allotments. Surplus reservation lands totaling over 2 million acres were opened to white settlement by lottery. In 1908, additional allotments made from some reserved pasture lands were granted to tribal members born between 1903 and 1908 (Brant 1969: 16). The allotments were generally well chosen, selected for the availability of permanent water, timber, and land suitable for pasture or cultivation. The Plains Apache allotments were distributed in a checkerboard pattern from south of the Washita River between Fort Cobb and Carnegie to along East Cache Creek and Tahoe Creek near the Alden, Hatchetville, and Boone communities.

The Plains Apache have generally fared as well (or as poorly) as other Indian groups in western Oklahoma since allotment in severalty. Although the U.S. government repeatedly encouraged the Indians to farm, few individuals were ever able to support themselves and their families from this activity alone. Gradually most families became dependent for their livelihood upon the income derived from leasing their unused lands to non-Indians. Many allotments passed out of Indian ownership as inherited lands were sold. The remaining Indian lands moved into fractionated heirship status, with a number of heirs of an original allottee sharing in the income from a tract of leased land. Increasingly, Plains Apache families faced the challenge of having to enter a labor market in which few opportunities existed for Indian people in western Oklahoma. A few families were enriched temporarily when oil was discovered on their allotments, but most gravitated to the lower income brackets of their local communities.

THE PLAINS APACHE IN THE TWENTIETH CENTURY

Plains Apache numbers decreased in the late nineteenth and early twentieth centuries, much of the decrease being due to diseases such as measles and tuberculosis. Indian Agency figures (Schweinfurth 2002: 24) indicate that the population was 332 in 1880, 241 in 1892, and 173 in 1909. The number rose to 400 in 1949, and the population continued to increase in succeeding decades, especially after 1987, when the qualifying blood quantum for tribal membership was lowered to one-eighth. By 2001 there were at least two thousand persons on the tribal rolls (Schweinfurth 2002: 24).

Tribal members are concentrated in southern Caddo County, Oklahoma, in and about the communities of Anadarko, Fort Cobb, Apache, and Boone. Others live away from the area in other towns and cities in Oklahoma and also out of the state. Those members living far away usually maintain close contact with their extended families in Oklahoma, returning often for the annual Blackfeet Dance or other special occasions.

The Plains Apache language seems to be on the verge of disappearance. The last elder to speak the language with any fluency died in February of 2008. The tribe has sponsored several language programs in an effort to save and rehabilitate the language, but their ultimate success is doubtful.

In the latter part of the twentieth century, the Plains Apache attracted much attention in their area through the Blackfeet Dance, a modern version of the traditional Manatidie society dance. The dance was revived in 1958 for the express purpose of providing a distinctive activity with which all Plains Apache could identify (Bittle 1962). An Apache Blackfeet Society was formed, and the revived ceremonial dance was alternately called the Manatidie or the Blackfeet Dance. It was hoped that this organization would serve as a rallying point for tribal unity and action toward common goals. However, the Blackfeet Society split into two rival Blackfeet Societies in 1964, each headed by a large extended family. Thus, the hoped-for potential for concerted group action has remained largely unrealized, although the sense of tribal identity has been preserved and strengthened.

Each dance group holds a three- or four-day annual celebration in the summer and performs the Blackfeet Dance upon request at various Indian community functions throughout the year. Because of its distinctive songs, dance steps, and attractive costuming, the dance is much in demand as a special attraction at the powwows of other tribes and at intertribal gatherings. The four fur-wrapped staffs are still the focal point of the dance, and certain ceremonial features are observed. The dance is used as a vehicle to honor veterans and servicemen, but mainly it serves as a form of entertainment and social interaction through which the Plains Apache feel that they share in a unique common heritage in which they can take pride.

For much of the twentieth century, the Plains Apache were represented by the Kiowa-Comanche-Apache Intertribal Business Committee, which handled the business affairs for the three tribes. This organization was dissolved in 1963, and the tribes began work on separate constitutions. After several years under an interim business committee, the Plains Apache adopted a constitution early in 1972, calling themselves the Apache Tribe of Oklahoma. Tribal affairs were to be executed through a business committee, members of which were elected for two-year terms. Subordinate committees could be named when needed to deal with specific matters such as health, education, economic development, and housing. A tribal complex housing business offices, conference rooms, and an auditorium was completed around 1980 and considerably expanded in the early 2000s.

The Plains Apache of today are the inheritors of a long Plains Indian cultural tradition that can be traced as far back as 1541, when members of the Coronado Expedition encountered the Querecho, a group of Apacheans subsisting on the bison and using dogs as pack animals. They entered the twenty-first century as a tribe, still increasing in numbers. Although facing serious problems in the areas of health, education, and employment, they remain firmly dedicated to preserving their connection to a unique cultural heritage.

This heritage includes a rich store of knowledge of the plant resources available to them in their several plains environments. Perhaps a great deal of this knowledge had been lost by 1963 and 1964, the time of the main fieldwork for this ethnobotany. However, the Plains Apache elders who participated in the fieldwork were extremely knowledgeable about the use of plants within the context of the traditional culture they knew and remembered. They had both observed and participated in the behaviors involving the use of plants, and, more importantly, they had access to information on plant use possessed by their parents, grandparents, and other older people in the community. They wished to preserve this information—this part of the Plains Apache heritage—for future generations of their people, as well as for others interested in the history and culture of American Indian peoples.

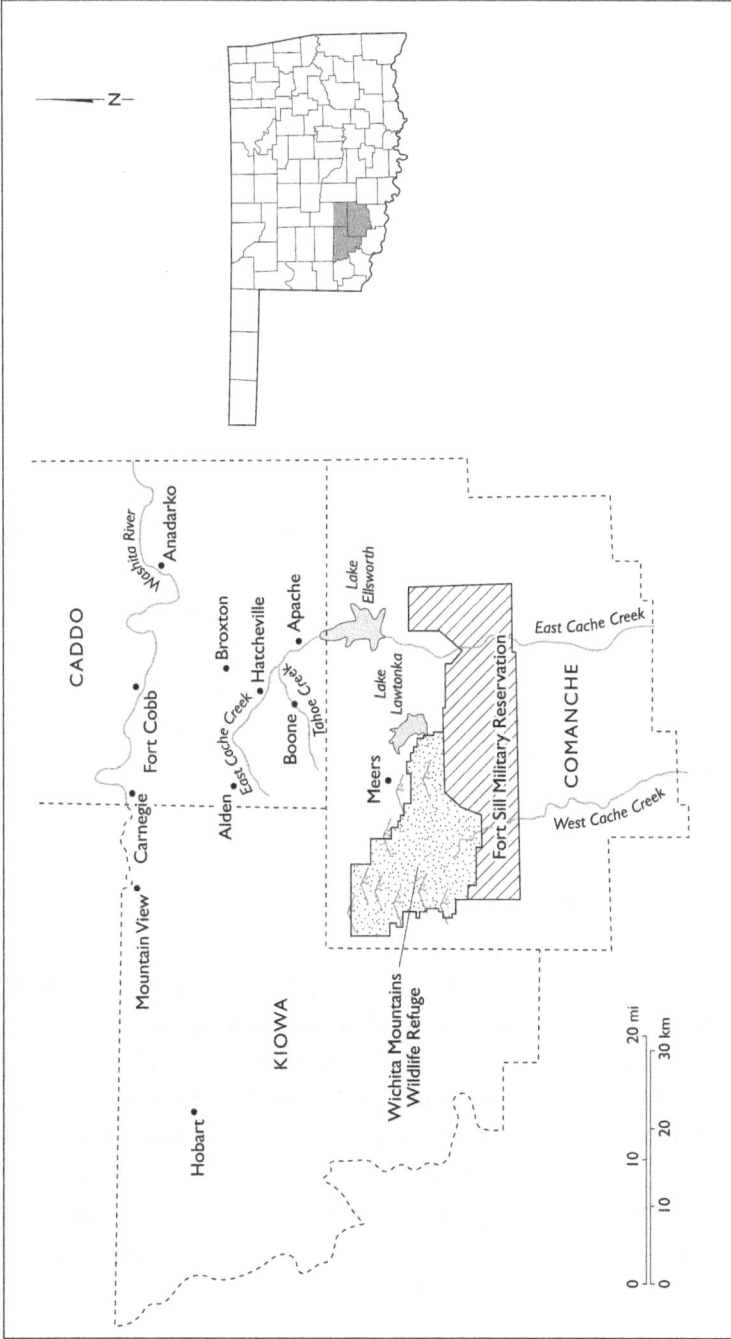

Area of Plains Apache residence in Oklahoma, 1963–65.

CHAPTER 2

The Plains Apache Plant World

THE SETTING

The ethnobotanical heritage of the Plains Apache is based on the Great Plains region of North America. The Great Plains extends over a vast area from southern Canada into central Texas and from the Rocky Mountains to the eastern deciduous forests, and it includes that area of western Oklahoma in which the Apache currently reside. The plains topography is generally one of low relief, with an eastward slope that ranges from about 5,500 feet (1,676 meters) to 1,500 feet (457 meters). The climate is characterized by hot summers, cold winters, and sparse annual precipitation averaging from ten inches in the west to a little over thirty inches on the eastern margin.

Contrary to popular belief, the plains are not uniformly flat, treeless, and featureless. True, there are sweeping expanses of nearly level to gently undulating grasslands. But the terrain is dissected by broad, shallow river valleys that may have escarpments, buttes, narrow canyons, deep ravines, draws, low hills, and fringes of timber along watercourses. In addition, the area includes some minor mountain groups, such as the Wichita Mountains of Oklahoma, the Laramie and Bear Lodge mountains of Wyoming, and the Black Hills of South Dakota. These features make possible a diversity of habitats, with corresponding varied assemblages of native plants and animals. The Plains Apache, who roamed widely over the Great Plains in former times, were no doubt intimately acquainted with the many natural resources of the region.

The natural vegetation of the Great Plains is dominated by grasses, with the short-grasses, such as buffalo grass (*Bouteloua dactyloides*) and blue grama (*Bouteloua gracilis*), being found throughout the western third of the area where rainfall is minimal. Tallgrass prairie is found along the wetter, eastern edge of the plains, where it intermingles with stands of deciduous forests. The dominant tallgrasses are big bluestem (*Andropogon gerardii*), little bluestem (*Schizachyrium scoparium*), Indiangrass (*Sorghastrum nutans*), and switchgrass (*Panicum virgatum*). In between are mixed-grass prairies, which are transitional zones and contain blends of tall- and short-grass species. In the past, all of these and other grasses supported the vast herds of buffalo upon which the Plains Apache, and other Plains tribes, primarily subsisted. These grasses were important also as pasturage for the large herds of horses maintained by the tribes in historic times. The Plains Apache no doubt recognized which grasses were important as fodder, but investigation into this aspect of their knowledge of useful plants was not part of this study.

The Plains Apache territory in southwestern Oklahoma is in the general area surrounding the juncture of southern Caddo, northern Comanche, and eastern Kiowa counties. This area has a rolling topography with elevations ranging from 1,200 to 1,500 feet (366 to 457 meters), although some elevations in the Wichita Mountains reach to approximately 2,400 feet (732 meters). The native vegetation is characteristic of a mixed-grass prairie, with some woodland and riverine forest areas. The woodland includes the western branch of the Cross Timbers, a band of forest intermixed with tallgrass prairie that extends south from central Oklahoma into Texas and in which the dominant trees are post oak (*Quercus stellata*) and blackjack oak (*Q. marilandica*). The riverine forest harbors such species as burr oak (*Q. macroparpa*), American elm (*Ulmus americana*), black walnut (*Juglans nigra*), cottonwood (*Populus deltoides*), and pecan (*Carya illinoinensis*). Most of this territory has been greatly altered from its original state through agriculture and stock raising. However, remnants of the original plant cover remain, most notably in the Wichita Mountain Wildlife Refuge and the adjacent Fort Sill Military Reservation.

Prairie landscape near Fort Cobb, Oklahoma, 1968.

RELATION OF PEOPLE TO NATURE

Plants were not conceptualized by the Apache as a distinct entity but were rather considered to be integral parts of the physical environment, which was accepted as given, natural, and correct in the basic order of things. In this view, there was an inherent harmony and balance in nature that was basically healthy and would provide endless generations with a comfortable livelihood. But there was no division of nature into conceptual realms such as the vegetable, animal, and mineral kingdoms. There was no word equivalent to the English "plant," although there were general terms for a few categories of native plants.

Bison and grassland, Wichita Mountains Wildlife Refuge, 1963.

The Apache regarded themselves as a prairie people, at home any place up and down the length and breadth of the high plains and the mixed grass plains but forever out of place and alien in adjacent mountains, deserts, and wooded country. Even the larger river valleys, such as the Washita and Canadian systems, which dissected the plains from northwest to southeast, made them feel uncomfortable, with their hot, humid microclimates in summer, their stands of heavy timber, and their distinctive complex of sand-loving plants. Many of the traditional stories retold by older people began with words like, "Way back, the people were roaming around on the prairie . . ." This preference for the high, open country, in contrast to the humid, sandy river valleys, could be seen

Plains Apache house near Fort Cobb, Oklahoma, 1968.

at the time of this study in the placement of Apache houses upon the lands originally allotted to them. Typically the houses were located at the crest of a treeless hill or ridge, often the highest point on the allotment, where an uncluttered view of the rolling prairie, with its grassy swells and timbered creeks and draws, extended for miles in every direction.

The Apache believed that all the native floral and faunal forms existed for the well-being of humanity. Every plant was regarded as potentially useful in some way or another. "That weed looks like it ought to be good for something" or "Every plant's got a use if you just know what it is" were common statements from all the elders. They regarded plants as good, valuable, and beautiful to the degree that they served a purpose in a cultural context.

Interestingly, the notion that all plants are potentially useful did not seem to apply to plants of recent introduction that have, in some cases, replaced or crowded out some native species. The Apache elders in our study tended to minimize or completely ignore such plants, both weedy invaders of disturbed or overgrazed lands and certain useful plants such as those deliberately planted in shelterbelts or for ornamental purposes. For example, even though Ray was a very knowledgeable elder, he was unable to identify a specimen of catalpa (*Catalpa speciosa*), a tree native to eastern Oklahoma that has been planted in Caddo County for years by white farmers and ranchers for harvesting as fence posts. Connie May once adamantly refused to identify a fresh specimen of bois d'arc (*Maclura pomifera*), a culturally very important tree for the Plains Apache, which was picked from a shelterbelt planting near her allotment. Even when shown its unmistakable and characteristic fruit, the "horse apple" or "Osage orange," she said, "I don't know it—that's some kind of white man's tree."

The idea of deliberate tampering with nature, for any purpose, was not a concern for the Apache. They made no conscious effort to cultivate or propagate useful native plant species (though many a plum thicket must have arisen from a pile of discarded plum pits), and they paid little or no attention to conservation of valued, hard-to-find plants.

With this attitude, it is not surprising that most of the older Apache exhibited a singular disregard or ignorance of the causes and seriousness of erosion and a corresponding lack of enthusiasm for preventing it. Fred once commented that during the decade of the thirties, the U.S. government had offered to plant a shelterbelt of suitable trees along the border of his land, but he had refused to accept the offer because it seemed to him like a waste of too much land.

The Plains Apache elders we interviewed recognized, in a general way, the changes that had taken place in the original plant cover as a result of plowing, fencing, and overgrazing. But to them these changes were but signs of the passing of the old order of things, the disruption of the balance and harmony of nature, and the elimination of all things Indian by the white man. They interpreted the severely eroded upland

areas encountered in many parts of Caddo County not as signs of serious
and perhaps irreparable misuse of the land by Indian and white residents
alike but as one more instance of the white man's destruction of a cherished former way of life. The elders would occasionally talk heatedly
and at length about the differences between the common plant species
of their childhood days—all of them useful and desirable, such as big
and little bluestem (*Andropogon gerardii* and *Schizachyrium scoparium*)
and other good grazing grasses, native edible tubers, and certain medicinal plants—and those they would maintain are the dominant plants
today—Johnsongrass, sunflowers, cockleburs, bull nettle, and other
introduced or weedy native plants that have become far more abundant
with changing land use patterns. Unfortunately, their words carried a
ring of truth, as these plants were common on roadside right-of-ways
and in overgrazed and eroded fields at the time of this study.

Included in the body of practical information the elders offered was
knowledge of the growth habits and distribution features of significant
plants. The Plains Apache recognized two major land types in their
Oklahoma territory, which they called, in English, "sandy land" and "tight
land." The sandy land, with its light, loose, reddish soils, was found
along the Washita River and its tributaries and included country in the
vicinity of Fort Cobb, Carnegie, and Anadarko. The tight land, with its
dark-colored, heavier soils, included the northern subsurface extension
of the Wichita Mountain region, which appeared as short-grass plains
with rolling topography. This country, encountered west of the town of
Apache and locally referred to as the "slick hills," has a limestone subsurface many layers thick that in places is tilted so that the various layers
are seen as parallel rows of rock where they intersect with the ground
surface. The Apache regarded tight land as normal and much more
common over the earth than sandy land. Ray expressed the feeling thus:
"Tight lands is just natural. The Apaches say that the whole world is
tight land. When you refer to the land, they just assume that the whole
earth is made of gumbo. Sand is foreign." The Apache term for "tight
land" (*'áánǫǫhéé*) incorporated the morpheme for "ground" (*-nǫ*) and
could be literally translated as "that of which the earth is."

The Apache elders knew well the kinds of plants to be found in
each part of their territory, and for some species they considered the

plants growing in certain localities to be superior to those of the same species growing in other places. For example, the leaves from "mountain cedars" (*Juniperis pinchotii*) growing on a particular mountain in eastern Kiowa County were reputed to be especially fragrant and therefore desirable for use as incense in peyote meetings and other ritual contexts. According to Ray, some clumps of sage (*Artemisia ludoviciana*) had a better than average odor and were preferred for ritual purposes. And certain plum thickets (*Prunus* sp.) were observed to produce larger, juicier, and sweeter fruits than others. Whenever stands of useful plants with especially good qualities were found, they were remembered and visited year after year.

Many of the culturally significant plants grew in both "tight land" and "sandy land," but some were distinctive of each region. Most adult Apache knew enough about the growth habits and associations of plants to find most items easily, even in unfamiliar terrain. In the sandy country there were occasional stands of blackjack and post oak in the uplands (the westernmost division of the Cross Timbers), which were interspersed with stands of big and little bluestem, Indian tea (*Lespedeza capitata*), chinkapin oak (*Q. muehlenbergii*), and thickets of plum (*Prunus* sp.) and sumac (*Rhus* sp.). Tall, straight cedars (*Juniperus virginiana*), with trunks suitable for tipi poles or fence posts, were ubiquitous in most of the region, especially in the well-watered draws and creek valleys. On the other hand, the shrubby, gnarled cedars of irregular shape (*Juniperus pinchotii*) whose leaves were valued for incense grew only on the dry, calcareous slopes of the "slick hills" in the northern region of the Wichita Mountains. Stands of western soapberry (*Sapindus saponaria*), persimmon (*Diospyros virginiana*), plum (*Prunus* sp.), and skunkbush (*Rhus aromatica*), grew in draws and depressions. Indian turnip (*Pediomelum esculentum*) was found in the dry soils of the "tight land," whereas Indian potato (*Apios americana*) was to be found only along the steep banks of major creeks. Strips of timber composed mainly of elm (*Ulmus* sp.), oak (*Quercus* sp.), walnut (*Juglans nigra*), pecan (*Carya illinoinensis*), mulberry (*Morus rubra*), and hackberry (*Celtis laevigata*) bordered the creeks and watercourses, and in the shade of the larger trees were dogwood (*Cornus drummondii*), grapes (*Vitis* sp.), black haw (*Viburnum rufidulum*), fall plum (*Prunus mexicana*), and chittamwood (*Sideroxylon lanuginosum*). Willow

(*Salix* sp.) grew wherever there was water. A few plants, such as sneeze-weed (*Helenium* sp. or *Boebera papposa*), were associated with prairie dog towns or former buffalo wallows.

APACHE PLANT NAMES

Although achieving a detailed understanding of the linguistic structure of Apache ethnobotanical terms was not the focus of this work, some generalizations may be made. As might be expected of a hunting and gathering group, the Plains Apache were unconcerned about plant repro-duction and did not have a detailed classification of plant parts. There was no term for "flower." The elders usually referred to a conspicuous inflorescence by a term meaning "pretty leaf" (-*'ít'ąγátł'aγe*), but they usually did not notice a very small inflorescence at all. Rose said a person could also refer to any particular flower by a term meaning "the top of the grass is [color]" (e.g., *tł'o'biláka'iłkaah*—the top of the grass is white). The term for "seed," *'í.tse'*, was also applied to "rock" and referred to something hard.

There were no standardized terms for flower parts. The sepals, calyx, involucre, and petals were all called "leaf." Stamens, pistils, and pollen were not distinguished, although, depending upon the plant, they could be referred to by descriptive terms such as "thread," "seeds," "that which is on top," "than which is within," and the like. Thus, Rose called the stamens of a flower by a term meaning "that which is within the pretty leaf" (*'ít'ąąγátł'aγebíízhik'éebíts'aah*).

The terms applied to plant parts were descriptive of their physical characteristics. The term for "root," *sédįsγas,* meant roughly "anything on or under the ground." "Bark" was usually called *minázhtǫs,* a term meaning "its cover" that was also applied to the hull of a nut. Bark could also be called "its hide" (*binásléé*). The term for "trunk" or the main stem of a plant was also applied to the petiole of a leaf and meant "its handle" (-*bíkąs*). Branches coming off the main stem were called by a term that could also designate the offspring or descendants of a person (-*bích'ąądes'ayeé*). Terms for other plant parts were made up in similar fashion and were possibly not standardized. Rose called "corn silk" by an expression meaning "corn, its hair" (*datá'sidáákał*).

Fred called it by a term meaning "corn, its leaves have whiskers" (*dadá'bitaaɣó'*). The tendrils of grape and other vines were called "its string or rope" (*bítł'oł*).

Culturally significant plants were recognized terminologically with more or less standardized terms, most of which were compounded of primary nouns and/or verbal phrases (Bittle 1963: 86). Many plant names were descriptive of some physical characteristic or property of the plant. Examples of such terms, roughly translated, are as follows: "red grass" for big and little bluestem, "bitter grass" for western ragweed (*Ambrosia psilostachya*), "yellow wood" for western soapberry, "bumpy fruit" for Indian pickle (*Matelea biflora*), "hard seed" for hackberry (*Celtis laevigata*), "earth's wart" for puffball (*Lycoperdon* sp.), "old lady's toenail" for unicorn plant (*Proboscidea louisianica*), and "it makes your hand red" for giant ragweed (*Ambrosia trifida*). Other terms were indicative of the plant's use, such as "it makes the gum numb" for blacksamson echinacea (*Echinacea angustifolia*, used for toothache medicine), "to color the arrow" for pokeweed (*Phytolacca americana*), whose berries were used to mark arrow shafts, "arrow stick" for dogwood (*Cornus drummondii*), which was used to make arrows, and "weed they make horse out of" for Baldwin's ironweed or child's hobby-horse plant (*Vernonia baldwinii*). A few plant terms were unanalyzable primary nouns: *gɣad* (cedar), *jee* (chokecherry), *yéechoh* (plum), *dlah* (green alga), and *boh* (*Solanum* sp.).

Most plants not native to the area were summarily dismissed by the elders in our study as "white man's plants" and ignored terminologically. A few introduced plants, however, proved useful in Apache cultural contexts and had been given appropriate names. Sweet clover (*Melilotus alba*), for example, was called "grass, it smells," a term also applied to sweetgrass (*Hierochloe odorata*). Both were utilized as sachets to make clothes and bedding smell good. Johnsongrass (*Sorghum halepense*) was called by a term meaning "it resembles red grass" (referring to big and little bluestem) and was sometimes used like the bluestem grasses for mattresses and brooms. A plant of Asian origin, the tamarisk or salt cedar (*Tamarix chinensis*), was called "freakish cedar." It superficially resembled the native junipers but had none of their useful properties.

PLAINS APACHE PLANT CATEGORIES

Several distinct taxonomic categories were identified from careful inspection of the Apache terms for the various plants and plant parts. Such categories seemed to be classes of a generic nature, roughly analogous to the English terms "tree," "weed," "brier," "vine," "wort," "berry," and so on, which recur as components in the common names of many plants. The Plains Apache categories thus identified were *tl'oh*, "grass"; *xosh*, "thorny plant"; *jee*, "fruit" or "food"; *-t'ąą*, "leaf"; *-ch'ił*, "brush"; *-kǫ'é* and *–ch'ish*, "wood" or "tree"; *tl'oł*, "vine"; and *datįįzhił*, "tall nonwoody plants." The existence of other native generic plant categories is doubtful.

PLANT PAIRS

A basic conceptual feature of Plains Apache ethnobotany was the belief that plants existed in pairs, one member of the pair being the "real" plant and the other being its "imitation" or "mate." The elders in our study were hard-pressed to elaborate this belief in general terms; however, Ray described it thus: "When Noah built his ark, there was two of a kind went in—male and female. Indians didn't have that story, but they have a belief that corresponds with that. Indians are observant, some of them, but I believe they're two of a kind. . . . They seem to think everything like entered the ark is male and female. According to the Indians, it's similar. Their conception is like that. That anything that has to do with plants and animals, there's two of a kind, male and female. That's my conception." Rose's comment was more typical. Regarding a particular plant she said: "Every weed has got a mate. This is the mate to Indian tea. It's like tea, but it isn't the same."

None of the elders, however, gave any indication that members of a plant pair were conceptualized as male and female. Rather, they described one member of the pair as the "real plant" and the other member (which might consist of plants within the same species in combination with plants of one or more different species) as merely a "fake" or "imitation." The imitation member of the pair was sometimes called a "mate," but gender was not implied.

We encountered a number of particular examples of "real" plants and their "look-alikes" during the research for this study. The real plant generally corresponded to a single botanical species, but the look-alike might consist of one or a number of superficially similar species of plants. The degree to which look-alikes resembled their real counterparts botanically varied and perhaps depended upon the number of closely related species native to the area, as well as the cultural significance of the real plant. For example, the mate to Indian turnip, or large Indian breadroot, (*Pediomelum esculentum*) was largebract Indian breadroot (*Pediomelum cuspidatum*), a plant that belongs to the same genus as the Indian turnip and resembles it fairly closely both in general aspect and in details of morphology. At the other extreme, the mate to the child's hobby-horse plant, or Baldwin's ironweed, (*Vernonia baldwinii*) was hoary verbena (*Verbena stricta*). The members of this pair came from different plant families, the Asteraceae and the Verbenaceae, respectively, and they resembled each other only in general morphology, both being rather tall weeds of leafy stem and purple inflorescence. The look-alike for Indian perfume, or wild bergamot, (*Monarda fistulosa* var. *fistulosa*) comprised at least two other species of the same genus, *M. punctata* var. *occidentalis* and *M. citriodora*, as well as individual members of the *M. fistulosa* species that did not possess the valued scent of the real plant.

The Plains Apache, then, conceptualized plants as integral parts of nature. They had no single term equivalent to the English word "plant," but they did distinguish several broad generic categories. They identified most culturally significant plant species with fairly standardized descriptive terms based on primary nouns and verbal phrases. The elders had paid little attention to plant reproduction or plant morphology, but when pressed, they were creative in giving descriptive terms for various plant parts. The Plains Apache also believed that plants existed in pairs, each "real" plant having one or more "imitations." They believed that every plant was potentially useful. As people of the plains and prairies, they had a respect for the native plants that provided them with a variety of foods, medicines, and materials for daily living.

Part 2

The Useful Plants

I have classified the vascular plants of cultural significance to the Plains Apache into four categories according to use: edible plants, ritual and medicinal plants, plants used for material culture and firewood, and plants used for personal care and adornment. This is a classification of convenience that was typical of the way ethnobotanical publications were organized at the time of my research, and it does not reflect a native Apache classification of the plant world.

The plants are listed in the next four chapters along with detailed descriptions of the ways in which they were used. Within each chapter the plants are listed alphabetically by genus. The scientific names given follow the PLANTS Database (USDA, NRCS 2008). In cases where the nomenclature has changed, the older scientific names are given in parentheses preceded by an equals sign (=). The common names used in the database are also given, followed by other common names used locally or by the Plains Apache elders. English terms used by the elders appear in quotation marks. Apache terms for the plants, along with approximate translations, are given on separate lines following the scientific and common names.

Some information on the use of fungi and green algae is given at the end of the listing of the vascular plants in chapter 4, Ritual and Medicinal Plants. Fungi are no longer classified as members of the Plantae or plant kingdom, although they were considered to be primitive plants when this research was conducted in 1963 and 1964.

CHAPTER 3

Edible Plants

The native flora of the Great Plains include many plants with edible parts—fruits, nuts, seeds, bark, leaves, and rootstocks—which formerly constituted important components of Plains Apache diet. Knowing how to locate and process wild plant foods may have ensured the tribe's survival in times when bison could not be hunted. "When buffalo became scarce, these people had to turn to the smaller animals—deer, antelope, elk, and even rabbits, dogs, and birds for food. Then life was difficult; the men had constantly to hunt and the women to dig for roots and search for berries and fruits" (McAllister 1955: 100).

By 1880, the bison, a major food source, were depleted, and the basic diet of the Plains Apache underwent a major change. New staples were introduced through government rations and white traders. These included beef, flour, rice, beans, bacon, cornmeal, potatoes, sugar, coffee, and lard. Thus, in the late nineteenth and early twentieth century, the Apache relied to a great extent, as they did at the time of this fieldwork, upon beef, cereal grains, fats, and starchy vegetables. However, many Apache continued to use the wild plant foods available to them in Oklahoma. Jim Whitewolf, a Plains Apache who was born around 1878 and was the subject of Charles Brant's ethnography, said that when he was a boy living with his parents they had dried fruit and dried meat at every meal. They also ate rabbits, fish, and the eggs of wild turkeys and prairie chickens (Brant 1969: 52). The Plains Apache welcomed wild foods as flavorful and nutritious additions to a diet heavy in dried meat and starches, cherishing them, also, as foods connecting them to their traditional culture.

Many wild plant foods were eaten fresh and in season, especially fruits and nuts. A few, notably plums and grapes, were dried in considerable quantities for winter use. In earlier days the root of large Indian breadroot (*Pediomelum esculentum*) was dried and pounded into flour for trade or later use (see entry on *Pediomelum* later in this chapter). Some edible plants, such as Carolina moonseed fruits (*Cocculus carolinus*) and various milkweed pods (*Asclepias* sp.), were eaten only casually, much as many children nibble on wood sorrel (*Oxalis* sp.). Others, like American lotus tubers (*Nelumbo lutea*) and cattail rootstocks (*Typha* sp.), were known to be edible but were seldom eaten and not especially relished. Possibly they were used mainly when preferred foods were scarce.

The Apache elders had little to say about green leafy vegetables, except that they had learned from their white neighbors to eat pokeweed (*Phytolacca americana*), watercress (*Nasturtium officionale*), and the green leaves of another plant, not identified. The Apache name for the latter was *'ít'ǫdátł'ichéé*, and it was said to look like spinach. The closest thing to a native, above-ground vegetable that the elders spoke of and praised was yucca (*Yucca glauca*), the flowers of which were called "Indian cabbage." The balance of this chapter describes each of the plants identified as edible by the elders in our study, as well as a few plants remembered by the elders as edible, but for which identifications could not be made.

IDENTIFIED EDIBLE PLANTS

Allium

Allium canadense L. var. *fraseri* Ownbey. Fraser meadow garlic, wild onion.
Allium drummondii Regel. Drummond's onion.
Allium perdulce S. V. Fraser. Plains onion.
Plains Apache: *łįbichíłchinah*, "horses won't eat it."

Several species of *Allium* are native to this part of Oklahoma, three of which are represented in the specimens collected for this study. The Apache term *łįbichíłchinah* applied to all species. Wild onions were eaten both raw and cooked with meat. Connie May said people used to hunt for them when they butchered, to flavor soup. Onions were dug in the spring and early summer, when they could be located by their leaves and long flower-stalks, which died down after the plants flowered. They were always eaten fresh, never dried and saved. Wild onions were small (up to about one inch in diameter) compared to domestic onions, which were reputed to have the same flavor.

Apios

Apios americana (Medik.) (= *Glycine apios* L.).
Groundnut, "Indian potato."
Plains Apache: *γádaatł'ǫ́dée,* no English meaning known.
A specimen of this plant was not obtained in our study, but it has been identified on the basis of descriptions from the elders. Indian potatoes were dug and eaten in the spring and were reputed to have an agreeable taste, similar to that of common Irish potatoes. They grow along the banks of small creeks or around springs, apparently close to the water line. Gertrude described them thus: "Indian potatoes used to grow along the creek banks. One time when I was swimming I saw them in a line along the bank. They were about one and one-half feet above the water. The dirt had fallen away and I could see them there in a line."

The top of the plant is a vine that trails along the ground or climbs on low shrubs. The "potatoes" occur along the root, several inches below the surface of the ground. Sometimes there are four or five of them, or perhaps only two or three. They are round, about one and one-half inches in diameter, with dark skins. Connie May said her husband's aunt had prepared them: "The old lady used to dig them. I went with her when she got them. Got a bucket full. Brought them back and turned them out on a table outside. Let them get dry. Then wipe the dirt off. Cook them with bacon grease, boil them. When they're done put them in a dish, pour off the water. Let them cool. Then take the rind off, eat them. They're good. They're better than potatoes."

The tubers of *A. americana*, growing along its long, horizontal root like beads on a string, were utilized as food by all the Indian tribes living within its range (Gilmore 1977: 42), being prepared for consumption by either boiling or roasting. The elders indicated that "Indian potatoes" could be hard to find. Connie May thought that cattle might have eaten up all the plants wherever they had been pastured. It was believed that if a person ate large wild potatoes, he would sink when he went swimming.

Asclepias

Asclepias sp. Milkweed.
Plains Apache: No term collected.
The tender young pods of several species of *Asclepias* were occasionally eaten raw by children or adults when they were encountered on the prairie. The elders often referred to these immature pods in English as "the pickle" of the milkweed plant. However, the real "Indian pickle" was the green pod of *Matelea biflora*, another member of the milkweed family (see entry on *Matelea* later in this chapter).

Callirhoe

Callirhoe involucrata (Torr. & Gray) Gray. Purple poppymallow, cowboy rose.
Plains Apache: *tł'odí cheelebilaga'íłchi*, "grass grows flat on the ground, its top is red"; *tł'oyégos'eł'i,* "grass spreads on the ground."
Rose said that children dug the roots of this plant, which are about the size and shape of parsnips, and ate them raw. They were rather tasteless and adults never bothered to dig them.

Carya

Carya illinoinensis (Wangenh.) K. Koch. Pecan.
Plains Apache: *ch'íłxashéé,* "put it in your mouth and crack it."
Pecans were gathered whenever they were available and sometimes stored in a bag for later use. They were apparently not used in cooking but were eaten as a snack food. Today pecans are mixed with the pounded meat that is served at peyote breakfasts. Native pecan trees were fairly numerous along Cache Creek and its tributaries in southern Caddo County, but they probably did not extend much further north on the plains. At first glance it may seem unusual that black walnuts, whose meats are much

harder to pick out than those of pecans, were more often used to flavor dried, pounded meat. This is probably because black walnuts were more widely distributed over the plains, and the Apache did not often encounter pecans until they were assigned to their Oklahoma reservation.

Celtis

Celtis laevigata Willd. Sugarberry, hackberry.
Plains Apache: *tsédítl'itséé*, "hard seed."
This species of *Celtis,* locally known as "hackberry," is common along creeks and in well-watered places. The fruits of the hackberry are rather small, globular drupes (one-fourth to one-third of an inch in diameter) that ripen to an orange-red color in September and October. They are very sweet and have a flavor reminiscent of dried dates. They were highly relished by the Apache both as a snack food, or kind of candy, and as a flavoring for dried, pounded meat. Hackberries were gathered by the women, who sampled the fruits from various trees until they found the ones with the best flavor. Rose said she always looked for the largest fruits, the size of peanuts. They were laboriously picked, one by one, and the bad ones were discarded and the stems removed. Since the fruits are so small, it took quite a while to gather up a few handfuls. Many were eaten out of hand at the time they were picked, the flesh and skin swallowed and the hard seed spit out. Some people with good teeth chewed the whole fruit, seed and all. Hackberries were sometimes made into a sweet condiment that was a great favorite with the children. For this they were mixed with tallow or kidney fat, placed on a hide or piece of canvas, and pounded up fine, seeds and all. The resulting meal, moist and gummy, was molded into little balls for eating. Sometimes it was molded on the end of a stick and toasted over the coals. Rose said she still liked to fix this hackberry treat for her grandchildren.

Hackberries were especially valued because they were one of the few sweet foods available in the old days. They were sometimes added to dried meat and tallow and the whole mixture pounded up fine. This mixture could also be shaped into balls and eaten without cooking.

Celtis is apparently a genus whose populations grade imperceptibly into each other and whose varieties cross readily with each other. The above discussion applies to all varieties of hackberry found in Apache territory, including *C. occidentalis* L. and *C. reticulata* Torrey. Certainly the Apache considered all hackberries to be the same, although the trees in some areas were known to bear larger fruits than others. Rose also said that hackberry was one plant that was all alone—it did not have a "mate."

Cocculus

Cocculus carolinus (L.) DC. Carolina coralbead, Carolina snailseed, moonseed.
Plains Apache: *jełchíích'eh,* "red fruit."
The small red fruits of *Cocculus*, ripening in the fall, were sometimes picked and eaten, usually by children. Gertrude and Louise both said they had eaten them but that they did not have much taste.

Crataegus

Crataegus sp. Hawthorn.
Plains Apache: *bak'ach'iłt'aahi,* "tree you make arrows for."
The small, scarlet fruits of the hawthorn were eaten fresh when they ripened in the fall. Rose had heard that arrows were supposed to be made for the tree before the fruits were eaten. She had also heard that if the tree were "bothered" too much, it would die. Connie May said eating too many of the fruits would make stomach trouble. The hawthorn is apparently seen infrequently in southwestern Oklahoma; during our research it was encountered only once, along a tributary of Cache Creek. Specific designation of the specimen from this tree could not be made. It was reported by elders to grow in the vicinity of Fort Sill and along Medicine Creek in the Wichita Mountains to the south.

Cyperus

Cyperus setigerus Torr. & Hook. Lean flatsedge.
Plains Apache: *koyáátł'oh,* "water grass; *yagozháyądík'aadéé,* "it makes the baby skinny."

The tender white part at the base of the culm was eaten long ago, according to Louise and Ray. It was eaten raw or possibly boiled. Louise said that when a nursing mother ate this, it would make her child skinny.

Diospyros

Diospyros virginiana L. Common persimmon.
Plains Apache: *ts'íγíítzhįįhįįbíje'e,* "Osage fruit" or "shaved heads, their fruit."
Persimmon groves were fairly common on hillsides and in draws. The fruits were ready to eat when they were "dead ripe" and fell to the ground, sometime after the first frost in the fall. They were not dried or preserved. However, Rose said persimmons were sometimes stored for a short time by being packed in layers in parfleches, each layer of fruit separated by a layer of grass so that no fruits touched each other. They would keep for some time packed in this way, and those picked green would ripen. They had to be checked every day or two, and any rotten ones thrown out.

Escobaria

Escobaria missouriensis (Sweet) D. R. Hunt. (= *Coryphantha missouriensis* = *Mammillaria missouriensis*). Missouri foxtail cactus.
Plains Apache: *xoshdíszhot'é,* "round sticker."
Louise said that the red fruits were knocked off the plant with a stick and eaten fresh. She said they tasted good.

Juglans

Juglans microcarpa Berl. var. *microcarpa* (= *Juglans rupestris* Engelm.). Little walnut, western black walnut.
Juglans nigra L. Black walnut.
Plains Apache: *chįįshch'įįdą',* "base of the nose."

Both species of black walnut are native to Apache territory, with *J. nigra* growing primarily along stream and river bottoms and *J. microcarpa* scattered in moist locations along smaller streams and in watered draws on the prairie uplands. Both species produce edible fruits (walnuts), but those of *J. nigra* are considerably larger than those of *J. microcarpa* and were those mainly used for food by the Plains Apache. Black walnuts were gathered and stored, and they were often pounded with dried meat. They added a distinctive flavor that was much liked. The nuts were gathered when they fell from the trees and taken home, where the husks were broken and smashed by trampling on them. The nuts were then left to dry out, after which the husks were stripped off and the nuts placed in bags for storage. Connie May said that if the husks were left on, the nuts would get wormy. When needed, the seasoned nuts were cracked between two rocks, or with a hammer or an ax, and the meats removed with a bone pick. Sometimes they were mixed with cooked meat that had been pounded up, and often they were simply cracked and eaten as a snack food.

Lespedeza

Lespedeza capitata Michx. Roundhead lespedeza, "Indian tea."
Plains Apache: *dóba'ít'ąą,* "coffee leaves"; *kółízhį de'ít'ą',* "black-water leaves."
A decoction prepared from the leaves of this perennial legume constituted an important native beverage called "Indian tea." It is still consumed by traditionally oriented Plains Apache. The plant grows in sandy soils, often in association with bluestem and blackjack oak. The leaves could be gathered from about the end of June on through late summer. The whole stems were broken off a little above the ground, tied in bunches, and hung up to dry. In two or three days the leaves were easily stripped off and could be stored for winter—tied in a cloth or placed in a jar. Rose said she crumbled the dried leaves into small pieces and made sure they were good and dry before she put them away—otherwise they would mold. She also said that to make tea, she used four full pinches of the powdered leaves to a gallon of boiling water. This manner of measuring was used also in preparing some medicinal decoctions,

where four pinches of powdered medicine was added to boiling water (refer to recipe in entry on *Solidago* in chapter 4).

Other elders simply said that a handful of the dried leaves was boiled in a pan of water until the resulting tea became dark yellow or red. It was then strained through a cloth and was ready to drink—hot, warm, or cold. The older Apache seemed to prefer it warm rather than steaming hot. The tea was usually sweetened with sugar. Tea could also be prepared with freshly picked leaves, but a greater quantity was required to make tea of the same strength. Indian tea was relished by some people both between meals and at mealtime, just as many people today drink coffee or tea, but it was also thought to be beneficial to the health and was probably consumed in larger quantities when a person had a cold, stomach ache, or otherwise felt bad.

Ray had collected Indian tea all his life for his aunt and other relatives. He said that when the characteristic seeding heads turned brown, the leaves were at the ideal stage to pick. Louise, however, said the leaves were best when the plant was in bloom. The dead, leafless stems remain standing throughout the winter, and their round, brown tops are conspicuous, serving to indicate where the next year's crop of tea could be harvested. In the early summer *L. capitata* was sometimes difficult to recognize because without its characteristic seed heads, it closely resembles *Lespedeza stuevei* Nutt., another lespedeza that was common in the same areas. *L. stuevei* was regarded as the "mate" to *L. capitata,* the *real* tea, and was called by terms meaning "it resembles tea" (*dóba'ít'ąąbe'ę́ęside*) and "tea, its stem is short" (*dóba'ít'ąąbikąs'áłchide*). Explaining the difference between the "real" and "fake" teas, Rose said: "There's two kinds of this tea. The other one [*L. stuevei*] is smaller. It's short. This [*L. capitata*] is the tall one. This is the main one. . . . Every weed has got a mate. This [*L. stuevei*] is the mate to Indian tea. It's like tea, but it isn't the same. It's bitter."

Liatris

Liatris punctata Hook. Dotted blazing star.
Plains Apache: *'izétałjįįbíje'ée,* "crow food."
The root of *L. punctata* was known to be edible, but at the time of this study it was eaten only by children. Louise said: "We eat these when

we were kids. They take the root and peel it. Take the bark off and eat the inside. Eat it raw. It's good. In them days we didn't have bananas or oranges—it was something good to eat, them days."

Rose had eaten the raw root also when she was young, and she added that children still ate it. She said the roots made the mouth a little numb, somewhat like the root of *Echinacea angustifolia*.

Neither Rose nor Louise suggested that the Plains Apache collected the root in any quantity or that they prepared it by cooking. Yet Paul A. Vestal and Richard E. Schultes, whose fieldwork with the neighboring Kiowa was done in 1934, reported that the Kiowa formerly dug the roots in the spring, roasted them over a fire, and referred to them as an "ancient food" (Vestal and Schultes 1939: 61).

Julian Steyermark (1981: 1474) described the root of this species as being "carrot-flavored." Kelly Kindscher (1987: 143–45) commented that the roots of *L. punctata*, though edible, vary greatly in palatability. He noted, however, that the plants are widely distributed over the prairies and are extremely drought resistant. Thus, they would have been an important food resource in times when other wild plant foods may have been difficult to locate, and the Plains Apache may have utilized the plant to a greater extent in former times.

Matelea

Matelea biflora (Raf.) Woodson. Star milkvine, prairie angle-pod.
Plains Apache: *jédígyashé,* "fruit with bumpy shape"; *'izelígyahi,* "white medicine."
Although a pod-bearing specimen of this plant could not be located during our study, both Louise and Rose identified a branch of *M. biflora* as the "vine" of "Indian pickle." The Apache term *jédígyashé* probably referred to small protuberances or nodes on the exterior of the seed pod.

The "pickles" were ready in midsummer and were eaten fresh and raw. The green pod was split open lengthwise, and the layers of soft, white, immature seeds were eaten. Louise remembered gathering pickles by the bucketful in the pasture when she was a child; each plant had three or four pickles on it. Pickles are hard to find in present times because cattle reputedly eat the young pods as soon as they are formed on the plant. The specimens encountered in the field did look as though the tops had been eaten out. These plants grew principally in sandy upland prairies, fields, and pastures.

The immature pods of several other varieties of milkweed (e.g., see *Asclepias* above) were often referred to as "pickles" as well, and these were occasionally picked and munched. However, they were not considered to be real Indian pickles. *Matelea* is, of course, a member of the milkweed family, and the pods resemble those of *Asclepias* spp., but the vines are recumbent or trailing rather than erect.

Louise reported the root of this plant to have been used as a medicine. (See entry on *Matelea* in chapter 4.)

Morus

Morus rubra L. Red mulberry.
Plains Apache: *'idákxah,* no English meaning known.
Red mulberry was common in the timber bordering creeks and watercourses. The ripe, black fruits were gathered in May and eaten fresh. In recent times the fruits were sweetened with sugar and sometimes made into preserves, but in the old days they were apparently eaten just as they fell from the tree. They were not dried or stored. Mulberries were called by the same term as blackberries— *'idákxah* (see entry on *Rubus* later in this chapter). Ray explained that there were two kinds of *'idákxah*—the kind that grew on trees (mulberries) and the kind that grew close to the ground on bushes that had stickers (blackberries).

Nasturtium

Nasturtium officinale W. T. Aiton. Watercress.
Plains Apache: *koyá'ít'ąą,* "water leaves."
Watercress, a non-native plant, grows in abundance in fresh-running streams and springs. The Apache ate it occasionally, either raw, or boiled and seasoned with bacon grease. Connie May said she learned about eating watercress when she was young and her family was camped at a church. She thought watercress was good with pork or potatoes.

Nelumbo

Nelumbo lutea Willd. American lotus, lotus lily.
Plains Apache: *koháá,* "big nose hole."
All the elders in our study reported that the tuberous roots of *Nelumbo* were eaten in the old days, but only Connie May had ever tasted them. She said a Caddo woman once gave some tubers to her aunt, who boiled them and seasoned them with bacon grease. However, Connie May did not like them. Louise remembered hearing her grandmother tell about getting this plant food in the fall, when the days were cool. People would dive in the water and get it, she said. Rose said the tubers were about as big around as a person's thumb and that they could be eaten raw, like a radish. However, she may have been thinking of cattail rootstocks, which were eaten raw, instead of *Nelumbo* tubers, which had to be cooked.

Melvin Randolph Gilmore (1977: 27) described the harvesting and characteristics of *Nelumbo* in his study of plant uses by Indians of the Missouri River region:

> It is an important native food plant, both the seeds and the tubers being used. The plant was much sought and highly prized by the tribes living within its range. The hard, nutlike seeds were cracked and freed of their shells and used with meat for making soup. The tubers, also, after being peeled, were cut up and cooked with meat or with hominy. It contributes a delicious flavor, unlike any other.
>
> The tubers were harvested by wading into the pond to search for them in the mud with the toes. When found, the mud was worked away from them with the feet, and they were pulled out by means of a hooked stick. In shape and general appearance they much resemble a small banana. . . . *Nelumbo* tubers might be cooked when first harvested, but to preserve them for winter use they were dried, being first peeled and cut into pieces about an inch long. An anatomical feature of the plant body is a ring of tubular air spaces extending longitudinally throughout the stem. This characteristic also pertains, naturally, to the tubers and gives rise to a droll notion in regard to them. The Indians say that one who is digging these tubers must be careful to

refrain from snuffing through the nostrils, else the cavities of the tubers which he digs will become filled with mud and so spoiled.

The fruit of *Nelumbo* consists of nutlike seeds that ripen in late summer or early fall. In former times they were used to prepare a beverage known as "Indian coffee."

The Caddo are reported to have been very fond of *Nelumbo* tubers and to have treated the plant as a semidomesticate, introducing it into waters of the areas where they resided. They may have introduced it into this part of Oklahoma long ago. The Apache name for the community of Fort Cobb, *kóhạ́dídeséh*, means "long big nose hole." Some believe that this name comes from the fact that conspicuous amounts of *Nelumbo* used to grow in the vicinity, possibly in oxbow lakes formed by the meandering Washita River.

Opuntia

Opuntia macrorhiza Engelm. Twistspine pricklypear.
Plains Apache: *góshchiish,* "red sticker."
The succulent red fruits, or "tunas," of the prickly pear were eaten fresh and raw when they ripened in the fall. They were picked carefully, or knocked off the cactus with a stick, and rolled on the grass to remove the stickers. The seeds were spit out. Sweet and juicy, these fruits were apparently highly relished as snacks.

Pediomelum

Pediomelum esculentum (Pursh) Rydb. (= *Psoralea esculenta* Pursh.)
Large Indian breadroot, prairie turnip, Indian turnip, tipsin.
Plains Apache: *tł'otł'ạ́ạ́,* no English meaning known.
Pediomelum esculentum occurs throughout the Great Plains, growing on dry hillsides and prairies. It was an important wild plant food of the Plains Apache before and during the reservation period. The edible part was an egg-sized enlargement of the root several inches below the surface of the ground, a feature distinctive of this species of *Pediomelum.* According to Gilmore (1977: 41), the tops of the plants break off and

Gertrude Chalepah picking prickly pear fruits, 1965.

blow away soon after the seeds mature, so that the roots are then almost impossible to find. The elders said the plant was formerly abundant in their territory in Oklahoma, but that it had become scarce because much of the land had been plowed or grazed by cattle. They said cattle ate the tops off before seed was produced. However, Dr. Bittle and I collected several specimens of the plant on a tract of undisturbed prairie west of Apache, Oklahoma. I revisited the site in 1996 in the company of a botanist and again found *P. esculentum* to be present, but when I went to the site in 2007, I was unable to find the plant. In the intervening years the land had been leased to a rancher, who apparently had disturbed the native prairie and planted it with bermuda grass.

The use of *P. esculentum* for food by the Plains Apache probably extended well back into their bison-hunting days. Wedel (1961: 38) wrote: "[I]ts starchy roots were eaten fresh or dried for winter use by tribes throughout the length and breadth of the Plains." Tabeau, a French trader who spent the winter of 1803–1804 with the Arikara on the Missouri River, reported that several tribes from the southern plains, including the Plains Apache (whom he called "Catarkas"), traded horses, dressed deerskins, antelope skin shirts, moccasins, dried meat, and flour made from the prairie apple [prairie turnip] to the Arikara for guns, tobacco, and other commodities (Abel 1939: 158). He also commented that

> the wandering Savages [have] many nourishing roots, which often preserve them from death during the frequent famines to which they are exposed. . . . But the prairie turnip is the most common and is not only reserved for these occasions but is used much even in times of plenty. This root has almost the shape of a turnip. It is covered with a hard and very thick black skin which is easily detached and always removed whether the turnip be eaten raw or boiled. The women cut it in pieces, which they dry in the sun and afterwards pound and reduce to flour. They make of this flour a rich, nourishing, and palatable soup. All the wandering nations leave regretfully the districts where the prairie turnip grows abundantly and leave it, too, only after having dried great quantities of it (Abel 1939:97–98).

Although the elders of this study had no personal experience with drying and preserving the *P. esculentum* root, surely the Plains Apache did so in former times, as described above. All of the elders had eaten the root fresh and expressed a liking for its flavor. Furthermore, they valued it as one of their most important traditional wild plant foods, and one about which their own older relatives had often spoken. *P. esculentum* was, in fact, one of the few plants that figured in Apache lore. In one version of an origin myth, there were many Indian turnip plants growing in heaven. Buffalo were grazing on them and bit the tops off. Then the buffalo dug for the roots of the plants and made a big hole. A woman in heaven looked through the hole, saw the earth, and tried to get down to it.

Indian turnip was dug in May, or just before the flowers appeared. Gertrude said that by the time the plant was in flower, the roots had declined in quality and tended to be dry. Indian turnip roots were ready to be harvested before the flowers of *Yucca glauca* were harvested for Indian cabbage, also in May. The root was peeled and eaten raw. Inside it was crisp and white, like a turnip. The roots sampled during the fieldwork in June of 1963 were past their peak condition. They were pithy and a little tough, but they were palatable and had an agreeable, though mild, flavor. The roots were probably most easily dug after a rain when the ground was soft. Growing as they did in tight, rocky soil, they were difficult to dig, even with a pickax, when the ground was dry. Gertrude said her grand-parents used to dig them in the evenings, using a crowbar or an ax.

A related plant, *Pediomelum cuspidatum* (Pursh) Rydb. (= *Psoralea cuspidata* Pursh.), resembles *P. esculentum* closely in its superficial char-acteristics and was regarded by the elders as its "mate" or "look-alike." It has a fat, swollen root that is coarse and unpalatable. Above ground it differs most noticeably from the "real" plant in that its stems are less hirsute and are recumbent rather than erect. Today it is much more fre-quent in occurrence than *P. esculentum*.

Phytolacca

Phytolacca americana L. American pokeweed.
Plains Apache: *k'áábehíbéshee,* "to color the arrow."
The tender young leaves and stems of pokeweed were boiled and eaten like spinach, being seasoned with bacon grease. The elders said that the Apache had learned to cook pokeweed from white people. The elders did not think it had been eaten long ago.

Pinus

Pinus edulis Engelm. Twoneedle pinyon, pinyon pine.
Plains Apache: *neezch'į',* no English meaning known.
Although this tree occurs in Oklahoma only in the extreme western panhandle, pinyon nuts were known in the old days from visits to New Mexico and other Rocky Mountain states. They were much liked and

always eaten whenever they could be obtained. Sometimes visiting Mescalero Apache and other American Indians brought a few with them to share with their Oklahoma relatives, but they were never available in large quantities.

Another product of the pinyon pine, familiar to Rose, was a chewing gum made from the pitch that oozed from wounds on the trunk and branches. Where the pitch congealed it became hard and glossy. This was broken off, taken home and allowed to dry. For chewing gum, a small amount of the dried pitch was taken in the mouth and chewed until it became soft and pliable. The first juice was bitter and was spit out. Sometimes water was added to the gum to get the bitter taste out faster. Rose had chewed this gum while visiting relatives on the Mescalero Apache Reservation but had never gathered it herself. She called it *jałíchii*, a term meaning "red gum" that was also applied to a chewing gum made from a local plant, *Silphium laciniatum* (see entry on *Silphium* later in this chapter).

Proboscidea

Proboscidea louisianica (Mill.) Thell. Ram's horn, unicorn plant, common devil's claw.
Plains Apache: *gǫchełabedízhishé*, "horn"; *'íshjánabisheezhyǫǫ*, "old lady's toenail."
The unicorn plant has a distinctive crescent-shaped seed pod about four inches long, which turns dark when it ripens in late summer. Inside are rows of flat, black seeds. The ripe seeds were often eaten as a snack food whenever they were encountered. Fred said he had chewed a lot of these seeds in his life; he would chew them until the flavor was gone and then spit them out. He said they had a sweet taste. Louise also enjoyed eating the seeds, which she said were rather greasy. It was thought that eating these seeds would help build up the milk supply of a new mother.

Prosopis

Prosopis glandulosa Torr. var. *glandulosa*. Honey mesquite.
Plains Apache: *nádískǫǫde*, "it has a curved shape."

Mesquite, though more typical of the arid regions of the Southwest, extends into Oklahoma along the North Fork of the Red River and its tributaries. Some mesquite trees grow on the southwestern part of present Apache territory. Mesquite pods were valued because they constituted one of the few sweet foods available to the Apache in the old days. The pods were picked in late summer or early fall, when they were mature, and stored for later use. When they were needed, the desired quantity was taken out of the sack and pounded up on a hide, pods and all. Rose said that no more than necessary were pounded at a time because the surplus meal would mold.

Pounded mesquite pods were sometimes mixed with cornmeal and made into a mush or gruel about the consistency of thin gravy, which was eaten with a spoon. Fred recalled attending a peyote meeting where a mesquite mush was served for breakfast. It was brought by a Kiowa Indian, and Fred thought it tasted very good. He also recalled having eaten a mesquite gruel that either his mother or his older sister had cooked, but he was not sure how it had been prepared. Rose said the pods were pounded to a fine meal, almost like sugar, and then mixed with the cornmeal and cooked. But Louise said they were pounded just a little, then put in water and boiled. After they boiled down they were strained, and the juice mixed with either flour or cornmeal and cooked some more. Rose also said mesquite meal could be mixed and eaten with dried pounded meat, or with any food that was sour, such as plums, to improve its flavor. Louise said that sometimes people just cracked the pods with their teeth and ate the seeds raw as snacks.

Prunus

Prunus spp.
Plains Apache: *yéechoh,* "big fruit."
Both plums and chokecherries are included in the genus *Prunus*, but the discussion here will focus on plums because chokecherries appear only rarely in the present Plains Apache territory.

Plums probably constituted the most important wild plant food in the Apache diet once they were established on a reservation in Oklahoma. Several kinds of wild plums were abundant on the southern plains, and their fruits have, no doubt, been harvested for many years by all Indian groups occupying this area. Archaeological evidence indicates that the prehistoric inhabitants of the plains were gathering and eating them (Wedel 1959: 232). The Apache term for any kind of plum was *yéechoh*, "big fruit," but the elders in our study recognized three different varieties. Two of these got ripe in the summer and were called "sand plums" in English. The other was a fall plum, and because of its characteristic habitat, it was often called "timber plum." All of these plums were utilized in the same way, although the summer plums, which grow in dense, compact thickets, were more numerous and easier to harvest in large quantities. According to Connie May, a lot of fog in the springtime was an indication of a bumper crop of plums that summer.

Plums were both eaten fresh in season and dried and stored for winter use. When the plums were ripe, the women went out to the thickets or timber to gather them, collecting them in skin bags or simply piling them on a tanned hide or blanket. Later Plains Apache used pieces of canvas, gunny sacks, buckets, and other containers. Traditionally, men did not help with the plum picking, nor, indeed, with the collection of any wild plant foods. But in the period under consideration, men occasionally did help in this work, especially when they were not employed in other pursuits such as farming or herding cattle. At the time of this study, many Apache men would stop when they came upon a convenient plum thicket along the roadside, and if the plums were ripe, they would take a sackful home to their family. In picking plums, the slightly underripe fruits were gathered along with the fully ripe ones, as they were said to ripen in a few days.

The plums to be dried were first sorted and the wormy ones thrown out. It was believed that eating wormy plums would cause soreness in the body. Then the good fruits were washed and boiled until tender. The excess juice was drained off, and then the plums were turned out on a hide or piece of canvas and pounded to a pulp with a stone maul. Connie May described the process thus: "My grandmother had a hatchet, a rock about the length of my forearm. She had some kind of hide over the end of it—slipped over the end [of the rock] when it was green and dried on it. She used it like this [demonstrating up and down pounding motion]. For to put the plums on she used a cowhide dried over a piece of stump,

Annie Bigman picking wild plums, 1963.

like is left after chop a tree down, and this was cleaned after it had dried, and all that stringy stuff taken off."

When the plum pulp was uniform in texture and of the right consistency, it was shaped into little balls and flattened out like hamburger patties. These patties were called *łįchi'eebigó'sha'*, an Apache name that means "dog tracks." In former times nothing was added to the plum pulp, but during the period the elders recalled, flour or cornmeal was often added. The flour added body to the fruit pulp and made it easier to fix patties that would hold their shape. But some of the elders felt that the floured patties were more apt to become wormy while in storage.

Fred and Annie Bigman in plum thicket, 1963.

After the "dog tracks" were shaped, they were placed on a clean canvas or hide and set out in the sun to dry. The next two days were critical in the drying process, as the plum patties had to be tended closely, protected from insects and other pests, and turned often so they would not sour or mildew. They were turned several times each day and brought inside at night so the dew would not dampen them or some animal eat them. If it rained during the day, they had to be taken inside. Five or six days, depending on the weather, were required for the patties to get dry and hard. Then they were stored. Formerly they were placed in bags sewn from animal hides and hung up in the tipi, but later they were stored in flour sacks or bags of canvas and hung on the kitchen wall.

The dried "dog tracks" were prepared for consumption by boiling them in water until they were soft and juicy, adding sugar to taste. Before sugar was available, the stewed plums might be sweetened with flour made from pounded mesquite pods or mixed with chokecherries. Individual tastes varied as to how thick the stewed plums should be. Some people cooked them down to the consistency of a jam, whereas others preferred them the thickness of gravy, or very juicy. If flour had been used in preparing the plum patties, it would thicken the mixture when the patties were stewed.

In more recent times, Apache women have learned to can fruits and vegetables and to make jelly, jam, and preserves. During the 1960s practically all of the women who put up plums for winter did so by simply canning them, seeds and all, with or without sugar. It is doubtful whether dried plums prepared in the traditional way have been prepared for some years, although the oldest elders expressed a preference for them.

Three botanical species of plums, corresponding to the Apache categories, were identified during the research for this study and are described here briefly.

Prunus angustifolia Marsh. Chickasaw plum.
Plains Apache: *'ayééchohíi,* "native plum," or "our plum"; *yééchołíchiihi,* "red plum."

This is the other sand plum recognized by the elders. It is also called "mountain plum" when it is found growing in the Wichita Mountains. This plum grows on small, shrubby trees about four to twelve feet high, which often form dense thickets. The trees have long, sharp thorns, and care must be exercised in picking the plums. The fruits ripen in late June or July, the mountain variety maturing later than those of the sandy country.

Prunus gracilis Engelm. and A. Gray. Oklahoma plum.
Plains Apache: *kachiníízhaye,* "enter into another land and stay there."

This is one of the summer or sand plums, and its bushes form compact thickets, one to three feet high, in sandy upland pastures and at the fringes of stands of blackjack and post oak woods. These plums are smaller than the other varieties, and ripen in late June and early July.

The elders gave two explanations regarding the derivation of the Apache term. One was that these plums grow anywhere—in all kinds of country and in association with all kinds of plants. Rose explained it thus: "This plant is like a person. It will join any tribe. It grows anywhere with any kind of tree. It goes away somewhere and grows in the sand." Louise provided the second explanation, saying that the term came from the fact that people picking the plums tended to wander off, getting farther and farther into the thicket.

Prunus mexicana S. Watson. Mexican plum, big tree plum.
Plains Apache: *yééchogodádiłchohíi,* "plum that chokes you"; *yééchoyagozhikodít'ihíi,* "makes your mouth pucker."

The Apache names for this plum are descriptive of the sensation felt in the mouth and throat on eating the underripe fruits, which are very tart. The term *-dít'i* was used to describe the taste of both fall plums and green persimmons. This plum grows on small trees that do not form thickets but are found scattered throughout the strips of timber bordering creeks. These plums were supposed to be picked as soon as possible after they became fully ripe, which was some time in October. The underripe fruits were too tart and produced a disagreeable feeling in the mouth, but soon after they ripened they fell from the tree and quickly spoiled on the ground. The Apache considered this plum to be the largest and most tasty of the native plums. It was reported to make the best jelly and preserves. It could be stewed, pounded, and dried for winter use like the others, but considering its habit of growth, it was probably not collected in the same large quantities as the summer plums. In English, the elders called this plum "fall plum," "winter plum," or "timber plum." Sometimes it was called by an Apache term meaning "timber plum."

Prunus virginiana L. Chokecherry.
Plains Apache: *jee,* "fruit" or "food."

Chokecherries are rare in central and southwestern Oklahoma, but the elders in our study had heard of them, and some had tasted them. They were, no doubt, eaten frequently in the days when the Apache ranged north and west of their present territory, being dried and stored in large quantities, like plums. Rose said her aunt always bragged about chokecherries, saying they were so sweet that sugar was never needed. They were often pounded with dried meat. Louise had heard that choke-cherries were first dried, then pounded up in a stone mortar, mixed with grease, molded into patties, and set out to dry for winter use.

Quercus

Quercus spp. Oak.
Plains Apache: *sǫch'ił,* "star brush."
Several species of oaks are native to the southern plains. Louise had heard from her mother that the acorns of these trees were sometimes parched and eaten, but none of the other elders knew of their use as food. It is doubtful that acorns were consumed when more preferred foods were available, and Louise, herself, had never tasted any. Both Louise and Ray said that acorns were fed to horses in winter when grass was scarce or covered with snow. Ray explained that acorns were mixed with cottonwood limbs and fed to horses to keep them fat in winter.

The Plains Apache term for acorns is *sǫch'iłbíje'ée.*

Rhus

Rhus aromatica Aiton. Fragrant sumac, skunkbush, skunkberries.
Plains Apache: *chédeek'oshéé,* "bitter seed."
Thickets of this plant are common on the hillsides and uplands of both tight and sandy country. The plants bear clusters of small, globular fruits that ripen to a rich red color in June. These fruits, locally known as "skunkberries," were made into a sauce that was consumed as a kind of condiment along with the main meal or eaten as dessert.

To gather them, a hide or canvas was spread on the ground and the berries were picked or knocked onto it. They were taken back to camp and sorted, and the wormy and shriveled ones discarded. Louise remembered that this sorting had been her duty as a child, and she found it very tedious. The berries were then washed and either dried or cooked at once. They apparently dried quickly and with a minimum of attention. Louise said they could be put in a sack and hung up, and they would dry with just an occasional stirring. Connie May said she dried them in the air first and then stored them in a flour sack or canvas bag. She said the berries would get wormy if left in a paper sack.

Fresh and dried skunkberries were prepared the same way. They were pounded on a canvas and then placed in a pot with water and boiled until tender. When they were done, the seeds and skins were strained out and discarded. The juice was then seasoned with grease, thickened with a little flour or cornmeal, and sweetened to taste with sugar. Connie May said that tallow or kidney fat was the grease used in the old days. This tangy sweet-sour sauce was apparently highly relished and was still prepared on occasion at the time of the interviews.

Ribes

Ribes aureum Pursh var. *villosum* DC. Golden currant.
Plains Apache: No term collected.
Although *Ribes aureum* is native to at least some portions of the southern plains, it is not common in this part of Oklahoma and was not important to the Apache. Louise recognized the plant and knew it by the English name, "currant," but she could not remember the Apache term. She recalled having eaten currants as a child but could not remember ever hearing her mother talk about them.

Gertrude spoke of some wild berries called *nádízhǫde* that she and other children used to pick and eat. The berries were blue, had two or three seeds, and grew on bushes similar to plum bushes but did not have stickers. The berries were about the size of wild grapes, and she said they tasted good. From her description it seems likely that these were golden currant fruits.

Rubus

Rubus sp. Blackberry.
Plains Apache: *'idákxah,* no English meaning known.
Blackberries were mixed with sugar and eaten fresh or made into jam or jelly. They were never dried. The Plains Apache term for blackberry, *'idákxah,* was applied also to mulberry. Blackberries were apparently less common than mulberries, and the elders gave us the impression

that while mulberries were sought out and gathered up when they were ripe, blackberries were eaten only if they were encountered ripe in a convenient place. Blackberry root was used for medicinal purposes (see *Rubus*, chapter 4).

Silphium

Silphium laciniatum L. Compassplant.
Plains Apache: *jáłíchii,* "red gum."
The sap of this plant exudes from the nodes on the stalk in September and October, forming large lumps. This sticky, waxy substance was gathered and chewed for gum. It had a bitter taste. Before modern chewing gum became available, this native gum was used by Indian doctors to close the aperture of the horn used in the cupping treatment, a doctoring treatment used to extract "bad blood" from an infected wound or an area where small cuts had been made to relieve pain. The large end of the cupping horn was placed over the area that had been cut, and a vacuum was created by sucking from the small end. When the vacuum was judged sufficient, the aperture was closed with compassplant gum held in the mouth and moved into position with the tongue. This kept the chamber airtight.

Sideroxylon

Sideroxylon lanuginosum Michx. (= *Bumelia lanuginosa*) Gum bully, chittamwood.
Plains Apache: *jełízhįdee,* "black fruit"; *-biɣagozakógezee,* "makes your mouth itch."
    The fruit of the chittamwood, a small, round, dark blue berry, was eaten fresh in season. Although the fruits are sweet, eating many of them was supposed to make the mouth itch. To prevent this from happening, the fruits were mixed with a bit of salt and set aside in a dish or bucket for several days. Then they were rinsed and eaten plain, without being cooked. Chittamwood fruit ripens in the fall.
    The gum-elastic, a clear, viscid substance that oozes from freshly-cut stem wounds, was used as chewing gum, though it had a bitter taste.

It was obtained by cutting away the outer bark and scraping the cambium layer or sapwood with a knife. Rose said the gum was mixed with a little kidney fat and made into a little ball that was chewed. The bitter juice was spit out. Louise said the gum was chewed with a mouthful of water to cut down on the bitterness.

Thelesperma

Thelesperma filifolium (Hook.) A. Gray var. *intermedium* (Rydb.) Shinners. Stiff greenthread.
Plains Apache: No term collected.
Louise identified a specimen of this plant as one used occasionally by her father to make tea. She said he and his men gathered the dried seed pods when they were out west hunting, and boiled them to make the beverage.

Typha

Typha sp. Cattail.
Plains Apache: *k'aazół*, no English meaning known.
The thick rootstocks of the cattail were known to be edible and were probably eaten on occasion. Connie May was the only elder who had actually tasted them herself. When she was a young woman, her husband once brought her some, which she ate raw. She said they tasted good.

Ulmus

Ulmus rubra Muhl. Slippery elm, red elm.
Plains Apache: *ch'iłjįį,* "black wood."
Louise said her father used to make tea from the inner bark of red elm. He peeled away the outer bark from the trunk of the tree and removed long strips of the inner bark, coiling and tying them up like a lariat while they were fresh. He used this for tea after it was dried. He cut off a portion of the dry bark and boiled it in water until the resulting decoction was dark, like tea. Then he strained it, sweetened it with sugar, and drank it. Louise said she had drunk some of it and thought it tasted good. She said elm bark tea was good for any kind of ailment.

The inner bark of red elm is fragrant and exudes a slippery, mucilaginous substance. The Plains Apache occasionally chewed it as gum. Ray said that at certain times of the year, such as in the spring when the sap was coming up in the trunk, this layer was especially sticky and good to chew. Connie May said a person could take a knife and scrape off a portion of the sticky inner bark and chew it.

Viburnum

Viburnum rufidulum Raf. Rusty blackhaw.
Plains Apache: *dadátł'itsée*, "dark blue."
Blackhaw is found interspersed with other trees along creeks and on wooded uplands. The fruit is a dark blue, oval drupe about one-half inch long. These fruits form in dense clusters at the ends of the branches and ripen in October. They were eaten fresh, in season, and highly relished because they were sweet and juicy. They were not dried or stored. All elders were enthusiastic in describing the fine flavor of these fruits, which in English they called "black hawk" or "black horse."

Blackhaw and chittamwood both produce small, dark fruits that ripen in the fall, and elders occasionally confused them in casual conversation. However, blackhaw fruits have flattened seeds, are dark colored all the way through, and are borne in thick clusters instead of being scattered over the tree. Chittamwood was much more frequent than blackhaw (see entry on *Sideroxylon* in this chapter).

Vitis

Vitis spp. Grape.
Plains Apache: *dáłts'ał*, "hanging in bunches."
Vitis riparia Michx. Riverbank grape, "summer grape."
Plains Apache: *dáłts'ał*, "hanging in bunches."
Vitis vulpina L. Frost grape, possum grape, "fall grape."
Plains Apache: *dáłts'ał*, "hanging in bunches"; *'ádałts'ałe*, "our grape" or "native grape"; *'idáłts'ałbíkosdídeesí*, "long-necked grape."
The Plains Apache considered grapes to be one of their favorite wild plant foods. They recognized two general categories of grapes: "fall

grapes" and "summer grapes," both of which produced fruits that were used for food in both fresh and dried form.

At least five species of grapes are present in the Plains Apache territory of Caddo, Kiowa, and Comanche counties in Oklahoma. Two of these species, *Vitis riparia* and *V. vulpina*, were identified during our study, but the fruits of all species are edible and could have been used by the Apache.

In addition to *V. riparia*, the Apache summer grape category probably also included *Vitis rupestris* Scheele (sand grape) and *Vitis cinerea* (Engelm.) Millard (graybark grape). Ray described summer grapes growing in rough, rocky hillsides in the Wichita Mountains along with mountain cedar. He said these grape plants grew out of the rocks and trailed along the ground, not climbing on trees. He added that these grapes ripened in June or July, were larger and sweeter than "possum grapes," made the mouth itch, and were called *nǫ'yáadáɫts'aɫ*, "ground-growing grapes." The above is consistent with data for *V. rupestris* in the Oklahoma Vascular Plants Database (Hoagland, et al. 2004).

Another summer-fruiting grape of the region, more widely distributed than *V. rupestris*, is *V. cinerea* (graybark grape), which the neighboring Kiowa used for food (Vestal and Schultes 1939). Although a specimen of *V. cinerea* was not collected during our field study, it is quite likely that the Plains Apache also used this grape.

The fall grape, *Vitis vulpina* (frost grape), is known locally to both Indians and non-Indians as "possum grape." It grows very tall by climbing on trees and tall shrubs and is common in wooded bottoms and in blackjack oak–post oak forest. Its numerous fruits ripen in October or November, with the largest clusters often borne high above the ground. Louise said that when she would go after grapes with her parents, she always had the job of climbing up the tree to knock them down.

The Plains Apache prepared and ate all grapes in the same way, though they did not find summer grapes in enough numbers to dry. Grapes were gathered when they were fully ripe (they do not ripen once they have been picked), and either eaten fresh or dried for later use. The manner of drying them was practically the same as for plums (see entry on *Prunus* in this chapter). They were first boiled until tender, and then the juice was drained off and the residue pounded to a pulp on a piece of rawhide. The pulp was then dropped by spoonfuls onto a clean board, hide, or piece of canvas or shaped into patties by hand. Some women mixed flour or cornmeal with the grape pulp, but Louise thought the patties were more apt to get wormy if flour was added. The grape patties were dried in the sun, being carefully turned and tended, as described for plums. When fully dry, they were stored in skin sacks and hung up in the house or tipi until needed. People prepared the dried grapes for eating by boiling them in water and adding sugar to taste. Usually they were boiled down to about the consistency of thick gravy. Flour or cornmeal in the grape pulp would, of course, thicken the juice some-what. Stewed grapes were eaten as a dessert; the seeds were spit out.

Yucca

Yucca glauca Nutt. Soapweed yucca, "Indian cabbage."
Plains Apache: *daɣígɣa*, "appears whitish."
For a short time in the late spring, yucca provided an important native vegetable food, its flowers being cooked and relished as "Indian cabbage." The flowers appear in late May. Although the blooming stage for each plant is short, the flowers lasting only three or four days, there is a period of about three weeks in which Indian cabbage can be obtained. To harvest it, several flowering stalks were cut and taken home. There, the flowers were picked off and cleaned. The tip end of the ovary (stigma) and the yellow anthers were removed and discarded because they would impart a bitter taste to the cabbage. The ovary itself, however, about the size and shape of a green plum, was cooked and eaten along with the perianth seg-ments, appearing as petals. In fact, according to Gertrude, "the green center part" was the best tasting.

When the flowers had been cleaned, they were washed and placed in a pot with water and heated. When the water came to a boil it was poured off and fresh water was added. Then the cabbage was boiled until tender, usually with some kind of meat to add flavor. Formerly, either dried or fresh buffalo meat, or perhaps a buffalo tail, was stewed with the cabbage. Later, bacon or salt meat was used, or simply a spoon-ful of bacon grease. Louise said her mother always dried and saved little

Louise Saddleblanket with *Yucca glauca* flowers used for "Indian cabbage," 1967.

scraps of leftover beef and added them to her Indian cabbage. But
Louise herself liked pork with it, in the form of bacon, salt pork, or ham.
All elders reported that the boiled yucca flowers tasted just like the
white man's cabbage, and they seemed to be very fond of this food.

The emerging flower stalks of the yucca were also eaten. Louise
said that her grandmother had told her that people used to cut the
immature stalks, about twelve to eighteen inches in length, and roast
the tips over hot coals until they were tender.

The mature seed pods were dry and inedible.

OTHER FOOD PLANTS

The elders described and named additional wild plant foods for which we could not, for one reason or another, obtain specimens. Although botanical identification is lacking, these were culturally significant plants. Some discussion of them may provide additional information on the extent to which plant foods were utilized.

One of these plants was called *kóyách'íłxąshé,* meaning "when you bite it, water splashes in your mouth." We did not obtain a specimen of this plant, which supposedly resembled a dandelion, because it blooms in early spring and has died down by summer, the time at which most of the plant collection was procured. This plant was reported to grow in bar ditches and other low places where water collects, or in moist, shaded places along creek banks. The edible part was a small, round ball, like a miniature potato (about one-half inch in diameter), that appeared on the root two or three inches under the ground surface. These little tubers were dug in early spring, about March or April, and eaten raw after the dirt was wiped off. The inside of the tuber was white and succulent, with a texture like a radish but without much flavor. These roots were not an important food item; rather, they were eaten mostly by children or by older people when showing their young relatives that the plant root was edible. Ray said it was hardly worthwhile to dig them if a person was hungry, since it would take too many of them to make a mouthful. This plant may be either *Krigia dandelion* (L.) Nutt., the potato dwarfdandelion, or *Pyrrhopappus grandiflorus* (Nutt.) Nutt., the false dandelion. It is definitely not *Taraxacum officinale,* the common dandelion, which is of European origin and has a small, straight root.

Another plant with an edible root was called *nádests'aaye* (Apache term not analyzed) or, in English, "Indian turnip" (although this is a different plant from *Pediomelum esculentum,* which was also called "Indian turnip"). This plant was supposed to grow on dry upland prairies, in the same localities as *P. esculentum.* The elders were, however, vague and inconsistent in their descriptions of the appearance of the plant top. Rose said it looked like an onion, having straight leaves and no flowers, but the leaves were not hollow like onion leaves. She said the root was dug, peeled, cleaned, and eaten fresh. Connie May thought the top of this plant resembled that of *P. esculentum*. She said her mother-in-law dug them, peeled them, and pounded them up and dried out the pulp. Then she cooked the dried, pounded "meal" with meat. This plant may possibly be longleaf buckwheat (*Eriogonum longifolium* Nutt.), which the neighboring Kiowa also referred to in English as "Indian turnip" (Vestal and Schultes 1939: 25). The description above, provided by Rose, approximates the general appearance of the plant.

Another plant we did not encounter during fieldwork was *sáaγód*, or Indian sweet potato. Ray had never seen it himself, but he remembered his older relatives talking about it. The edible portion was the underground tuber, which was reported to have a flavor similar to that of sweet potatoes. Ray had heard that this plant grew in the vicinity of present-day Fort Cobb. Rose said the top of the plant had stickers or thorns and that the leaves were "wooly." She said the plant grew in sandy country and had a long tuber, about the thickness of a man's thumb. She said the root was dug in the spring and eaten raw. The tops were chopped off before the roots were dug.

Rose also reported that the Apache used to eat the leaves of some kind of "weeds" that they called *'ít'ạdátl'ichéé*. She said that these plants grew along creeks and looked like spinach, and that they were eaten when the tops were tender, in May or June.

A few other terms and comments by the elders indicate that still other wild plant foods were known and used, but information concerning them is so fragmentary that they cannot be described.

CHAPTER 4

Ritual and Medicinal Plants

I have grouped ritual and medicinal plants together because Plains Apache healing practices were based on prayer and ritual, and medicines were both prepared and administered in a religious context. An exhaustive discussion of Apache beliefs concerning doctoring and disease is beyond the scope of this book, and Michael Grantham Bross (1962) has dealt at length with the Apache concepts of body and health. Yet I am including a summation of these concepts as a background for the discussion of plant materials used for rituals and medicines. A discussion of sweat lodges is also included in this chapter.

CONCEPTS OF HEALTH AND ILLNESS

The Plains Apache conceived of disease as a disruption of harmony between humanity and the external world. They considered most sickness to be the result of witchcraft, ghosts, or the invasion of the body by some evil force or foreign object. They especially feared "ghost sickness," caused by the visitation of the ghost of a deceased person with malevolent intentions toward the living. Symptoms of a mild case of ghost sickness were depression and bad dreams. More severe cases could be marked by hysteria, insanity, or paralysis, particularly facial paralysis causing a twisting of the mouth and eyes. Severe cases of ghost sickness had to be treated by a doctor or shaman with special powers to combat the ghost and restore health (Opler and Bittle 1961: 392).

The overall treatment of illness was designed to restore harmony and combat the witchcraft or agents of evil, as well as to relieve localized physiological symptoms of distress. Another fundamental and related concept was the belief that the individual existed as a psycho-biological whole. There was no dichotomy between mind and body, between the physical and the spiritual. Illness affected the whole person, and the whole person must be treated to effect a cure. These basic assumptions explain many of the patterned behaviors involved in the treatment of the sick. Thus, although particular medicines were prepared to relieve localized symptoms, they were administered with the aim of treating the whole person, mind and body, and restoring him or her to a healthy relationship with the external world.

In the Apache point of view, the physiological symptoms of disease fell into such categories as sore throat, broken bones and sprains, hemorrhage, stomach trouble, diarrhea, colds, headaches, rheumatism, rashes, swelling, and respiratory ailments. To this list, which is by no means exhaustive, could be added a number of nonindigenous ailments such as mumps, measles, smallpox, cancer, pneumonia, tuberculosis, eczema, and other diseases. Apache medicines were administered toward the end of relieving the symptomatic distress of all these disorders. But to restore health for the whole person, the prayers and rituals accompanying the medicines were equally important.

MEDICINES AND DOCTORING

A wide variety of native plants was used in preparing medicines. Many, perhaps most, Apache medicines contained at least one plant ingredient. Some medicines were prepared from a single plant only; others were concoctions of several ingredients and might include vegetable, animal, and mineral materials. The medicines discussed later in this chapter under *Cuscuta* and *Lithospermum* each contained four ingredients.

Most older Apache men and women owned a medicine bag (not to be confused with the sacred tribal medicine bundles) in which they kept their accumulated store of curing paraphernalia. The medicinal materials were stored in small individual buckskin or cloth sacks and tied up securely. Some of the medicines were mixtures of several ingredients, dried, powdered, and ready for use. Others consisted of the dried parts of single plants—whole roots, crumbled leaves, seeds, or flower heads.

Other items such as red paint stone (hematite), yellow clay, a cupping horn, slivers of brown glass, and various animal parts might also be kept in the medicine bag.

The dried plant medicines could be stored and used for years. Unfortunately, a majority of plants are unidentifiable when in the form of dried powder or pieces of dried roots, and so the elders of our study often did not know which plant materials were in the medicines their own elders had used. For example, Louise was able to tell of a number of medicines she had seen in her father's medicine bag, but she did not know which plants he had used to prepare them. Her description, and those of the other elders, would indicate that the Plains Apache possessed a rich store of knowledge concerning the medicinal properties of many plants, much of which had been irreparably lost by the time of this study. Nevertheless, a considerable amount of information concerning medicines and doctoring was recovered and is presented in this chapter.

The elders had all utilized both indigenous Apache and western medicines and seemed inclined to accept either one, depending on the ailment. We gained the impression that although the older Apache gave lip service and claimed loyalty to their traditional remedies, they were more apt to make use of Western medicine and sometimes combined the two approaches. For example, when Rose broke her hip in 1963 she went to a modern hospital, where the bone was set and she received medication. Along with this treatment she also applied one of her family medicines, a root that, when chewed and applied externally, was reputed to be good for the pain and swelling accompanying broken bones.

In the old days, doctoring a sick person could be done by a number of persons. For minor ailments, an older relative, possessed of medical knowledge and experience, usually prescribed the treatment. For more serious ailments or if the family medicine had no effect, a specialist might be called in by the sick person's relatives. The specialist would be a person known to have power and medicines to treat the particular disorder. Some medicines were known to practically every adult Apache, and were used freely as needed. However, other medicines were owned by certain families, whose members alone had the right to prepare and use them.

For example, Fred and Connie May, who were brother and sister, had a fever medicine that was highly respected by all the other elders. Fred said his father learned about this medicine in a dream, in which he was shown the plant required and how to prepare it. Since the origin of this medicine in Fred's family is known, its subsequent dissemination is an interesting illustration of Apache patterns of transmission of medicines: Fred's father gave the medicine to his wife and told her to use it after he died. She in turn instructed both her daughter and son, Connie May and Fred, in its use. She gave some of the medicine to Gertrude, her grand-daughter, but did not show her what plant it was or where to get it. Fred also provided Gertrude, his cousin, with the medicine on occasion, without offering to show her what plant he picked. Fred's wife, a Kiowa woman, could also prepare the medicine. She expressed her confidence in it and seemed very happy to get some of the extra stems that were collected during the fieldwork.

Family medicines, being the sole property of members of the family, could not be made or used successfully by outsiders. Louise, for example, said that even if she knew which "weed" Fred used for his fever medicine, it would not work for her since it belonged to his family. Rose said: "Just the owner of the medicine, it will work for him. You got to have your own medicine, then it will work for you." In another example, Louise described the ownership of a plant known as "white medicine": "My daddy didn't use this, but my mother did. He didn't use it because, like I told you, Indian medicines goes with families, and this medicine goes with my grandma. Those days you got to take your own medicine cause they say if the medicine don't belong to you it won't work. It might be a superstition, but I kinda believe it, myself."

Other elders also mentioned medicines that had come down in their families for generations. These medicines were usually in the charge of older members of the family, either men or women. It was believed that persons who had had much experience in dealing with sickness were most capable of preparing and administering medicines. The owner of the medicine could do whatever he or she wanted to with it. The owner might prepare small quantities to give to friends or relatives, along with instructions as to its use, or impart the knowledge concerning its preparation to a favorite younger relative. In the latter case, the owner would make the young person a gift of the medicine, including the right to prepare it and use it, and reveal all the beliefs and rules surrounding it.

The owner would probably take the novice out into the country and show the young person the plants and other materials needed and how to collect them. The owner was not obligated, however, to transmit the medicine to anyone. In the absence of a serious-minded younger relative, a person might go to the grave without ever revealing the knowledge to anyone. In such a case, the medicines, along with other personal possessions, were disposed of after the owner's death. Connie May, for example, stated that her mother's medicines were placed in her casket and buried with her. Louise said her father's medicine bag was thrown in the creek after his death. Sometimes leftover medicines were also disposed of by being poured on the ground in a place where no one would walk on them.

Rose told how a doctor in her extended family administered medicine to her grandson:

My grandson was bit on the leg by a water snake. There were two little spots where the teeth went in. They got kind of blue. We set him down on the front porch and he was crying. Old man Apache John came walking down the road. He knows something about medicine. We asked him to use his medicine on my grandson. He asked what kind of snake had bit the boy and we told him it was a water moccasin. He said he didn't know anything about curing that kind of bite. His medicine was only good for rattlesnake. But he said he would do something. He took some medicine out of a little bag that he carried with him. He told my daughter to get some chipped glass. He took this glass and cut across and across those two tiny holes. After he cut, he put his mouth on the bite and sucked it. He put some of his medicine in his mouth and chewed it up. Then he blew it on the bite four times. Then he put some medicine on his finger and kind of pushed it in there. That was good medicine—it worked.

In theory, any adult man or woman who had inherited certain medicines could use them to treat members of the family or even outsiders who requested treatment. In practice, it appears that one or two members of the extended family were especially skilled in nursing the sick, and to them usually fell the duty of preparing and administering medicines. Members of the family received their services without charge. Outsiders, however, were expected to pay for medicine or doctoring services. Payment was supposed to consist of a group of four items, which could either be of nominal worth or of great value.

Persons whom the Plains Apache called "doctors" were at least part-time specialists in curing and made a business of selling their services and medicines, in contrast to family members with medicines who might, on occasion, treat persons outside the family. Male doctors were usually shamans, or medicine men, who possessed supernatural powers as well as potent medicines and knowledge of healing rituals. Sometimes they specialized in the treatment of certain ailments, such as snake bites, stomach troubles, rheumatism, broken bones and wounds, and so on. Both men and women could become doctors, but women only rarely became shamans. Doctors received their curing powers both through supernatural revelation and through their instruction from an older mentor, usually a relative, in the use of remedies and curing techniques. They doubtless supplemented their knowledge with practical experience, and their reputations as doctors were confirmed by their success in curing patients. Doctors whose medicines had no noticeable curative effect or whose patients died suffered a loss of prestige and a subsequent loss of business, whereas successful doctors were highly respected and were often materially well-off as a consequence of the fees they received. On the other hand, successful doctors were also likely to be suspected of witchcraft.

Saddleblanket, Louise's father, was a well-known medicine man and doctor. He was both respected for his knowledge and ability and feared because of the possibility that he might use his powers to work "bad medicine." Louise, however, made him sound like the old-fashioned country doctor: "My dad was a doctor. Them days, they don't have money, but they give a horse or a blanket or anything they want to give. He could doctor anybody that came after him. They come clear out to our house, late at night sometimes. He'd hear a wagon coming or a horse trotting up, and say 'Here come some one,' and sure enough, someone would be after him for doctoring. He had lots of medicines, but I don't know all of them. . . . I don't know what the leaves of them is like." Louise added that he never refused to doctor anyone who asked him.

What the payment would be was usually left up to the patient's family, though the doctor expected it to consist of four items. His medicines were not supposed to work unless he was paid. Usually the family knew the kind of items he would prefer to receive and tried to give these things. A typical payment for routine doctoring service might be a sack of tobacco, a black handkerchief, an eagle feather, and perhaps, a coin. Horses, tanned hides, blankets, moccasins, and other articles of clothing were also suitable items. In later years money was given. Sometimes a doctor would name the things he wanted. If he did not want the case for some reason, he might name a fee so high that the family could not pay it.

In addition to administering medicines, several other techniques were used in curing sickness. The "cutting operation" involved making a number of short shallow incisions over a bruised or painful area of the body with a razor-sharp sliver of brown glass. This was supposed to let out excess blood, or "bad blood," and bring relief from pain. The "cupping operation" often accompanied cutting but could also be used alone. In this treatment, a section of buffalo or cow horn was used to suck away excess blood from a cut area or to remove foreign objects from the body. Sometimes the doctor sucked the patient's body with his mouth instead of using a horn. Gertrude had had a fish bone dislodged from her throat this way, and Fred said some small blood clots were once sucked from his chest when he had pneumonia. Other techniques included placing a black handkerchief over the patient's face, tapping the patient's head with an eagle feather, massaging the abdomen, and burning a short, slender piece of sage (*Artemisia ludoviciana*) on the skin as a counter-irritant.

All of these practices, including the administration of medicines, were performed with prayer and ritual. But treatment of serious illness or personal problems, as well as preparation for important tribal activities, might begin with a sweat lodge ceremony.

SWEAT LODGES

Sweat lodges were used for both medicinal and ceremonial purposes, as well as to cleanse the body. The sweat lodge rituals were considered to affect the whole person, both mind and body. Pain, sickness, and depression were driven out, and both body and mind were purified.

Long ago, sweat lodge ceremonies were sometimes held to fulfill a vow made at a time of stress. Ray's father said that a man whose son was away on a raid might promise Fire Boy (a Plains Apache culture hero) that he would build a sweat lodge if he returned safely. In such cases prayers of thanksgiving would be offered during the sweat lodge ceremony. Sometimes men underwent the sweat lodge ritual to purify themselves, to make themselves clean inside and out, before performing some sacred task such as opening one of the tribal medicine bundles. The sweat lodge might be held to communicate with the source of supernatural power, to find out what had happened to a relative lost on the warpath, or to learn about the movements of enemies from another tribe. Another purpose might be to petition the supernatural for power to do something to help one's family. All of these reasons were primarily religious in nature, but good health was also promoted and sickness warded off by participation in the services. These ceremonies were also conducted for the express purpose of curing a sick person. They were considered to be especially beneficial for cases of rheumatism, arthritis, and other body aches, for inside the sweat lodge one would "sweat the sickness away." Sometimes a man held a ceremony simply because he was depressed or just did not feel good.

Sweat lodges were usually built in the open, near a stream of running water. A small, low, hemispherical structure, a sweat lodge consisted of a framework of willow poles tied together at the top and covered with hides, canvas, or quilts. The size of the sweat lodge depended upon how many people were to use it. Usually no more than six men participated at a time, one of them being the leader, or sponsor, who, with the help of his wife, had built the lodge and provided the necessary equipment. Slender willow poles, about two inches in diameter at the base, were set in the ground about one foot apart, bent inward, and tied at the center. Strips of bark peeled from the poles were used to lash the poles together. The poles were set in a circular or ovoid floor pattern, with a space being left on the east side for the entrance. The entrance was covered with a flap of cloth or a pelt that could be fastened down securely. The object was to keep the structure as small and tight as possible so the steam would fill the space thickly and cause heavy sweating. In the center of the sweat lodge floor was a pit about two feet across in which rocks, heated on a fire outside, were placed on a bed of ashes. A place was prepared on which to rest live coals, which were used to light pipes or burn cedar leaves.

Water from a container kept inside the lodge was poured or sprinkled on the heated rocks to produce dense clouds of steam, which permeated the entire lodge. In the hot, moist atmosphere, the participants, naked except for a loincloth, perspired heavily. They hit themselves about the shoulders, neck, back, arms, and legs with switches of sage or bluestem grass as the steam enveloped them. This was supposed to make them feel good, as well as to help in removing the dirt from their bodies. Connie May said participants hit the places where the hot steam burned them, and this took the hurting away. Every now and then the atmosphere got so stuffy that someone had to lift the bottom of the cover to let in some air.

A certain amount of ritual might accompany the construction of a sweat lodge, as described by Whitewolf (1969: 121–22) in the following passage:

Apache John [a medicine bundle owner] . . . said that we should get up early in the morning and not drink or eat. He told us where we could find willow trees. He said that the first willow cut should fall northward, the second should fall eastward, the third should fall southward, and the fourth should fall westward. He said that after those four willows were cut in that manner, the rest could be cut freely. . . .

He showed me how to place the four willows in the proper directional places. I bent the north and south ones over at the top and tied them; then the east and west ones. Then I started by the south willow and worked around clockwise putting in the rest of the willows. When the whole framework was up, I covered it over thickly with quilts, which would hold the steam in. On the east side there was a quilt used as a doorway. John told me to get some horse manure and put it on the west side, inside the sweathouse. Then I placed a bundle of grass on the west side of the manure. Outside, there were two fellows, already stripped and fixing themselves grass switches to use in the sweathouse.

Participants in the sweat lodge ceremony were usually mature men, but women could use it, too, for sweat-bathing or to treat illness. However, men and women never used the sweat lodge at the same time. When the ritual was over, the covering was removed from the frame, which was left standing until it rotted away. According to Louise, children were never allowed even to touch the poles of an old sweat house, for fear they would become paralyzed.

RITUAL AND MEDICINAL PLANTS

Following is a list of the vascular plants used by the Plains Apache, presented in alphabetical order by genus. For each identified plant species the full scientific name as now found in the PLANTS Database (2008) is given, followed by the common name(s) and the Plains Apache name(s). In cases where the scientific plant names have changed since the time of our study, the older terms are also given. The older terms are included also in the index. Entries for the two types of fungi used by the Plains Apache are listed in a separate section following the entries for vascular plants.

Ambrosia

Ambrosia psilostachya DC. Cuman ragweed, western ragweed.
Plains Apache: *tł'o'dį́įch'iihi*, "bitter grass."
Juice obtained by pounding ragweed leaves to a pulp was used by Plains Apache people as a very potent, if painful, remedy for screwworms in horse wounds. Usually the leaves of this plant alone were used, but sometimes a small amount of salt was added, or some sage (*Artemisia ludoviciana*) leaves. The juice, either straight or slightly diluted with water, was stuffed into a cut or wound that was infested with screwworms. The horse usually had to be thrown and tied down for this treatment because the medicine produced a strong burning sensation. On a deep wound, a bandage was applied or a rag stuffed in after the medicine, which was left in the cavity several hours or overnight. When the rag was removed, the maggots were dead and either spilled from the opening or were removed with a blunt stick. If any maggots remained alive, the treatment was repeated. Healing was supposed to take place rapidly after this. This screwworm medicine could also be used on dogs, in the same way as for horses.

This medicine was considered to be too strong for use on people, though it was occasionally used as a kind of last-resort remedy on persistent sores. It was very painful when applied, and a decoction prepared from broomweed (*Amphiachyris dracunculoides,* see next entry) was usually used instead.

Amphiachyris

Amphiachyris dracunculoides (DC.) Nutt. (= *Gutierrezia dracunculoides* (DC.) S. F. Blake). Prairie broomweed.
Plains Apache: *bekózhǫǫshe,* "broom"; *tł'o'xéhach'í'a',* "grass, burns quick."
The tops of fresh, mature broomweeds were boiled to make a medicine that was applied externally for skin ailments and taken internally for lung trouble and colds. Broomweed is a common annual, blooming from August through October, at which time it forms a round, spreading crown covered with small, bright yellow flowers. The tops of the plants, including the stems and flowers, were gathered into a bunch, tied in a cloth, and boiled until the decoction was dark and strong. Then the solution was strained through a clean cloth and was ready to use. Rose said it was good for doctoring heat rash, sores, poison ivy, athlete's foot, and other skin troubles. The afflicted area was bathed liberally in the liquid as many times as was necessary to dry up the rash.

The medicine was also taken internally, like a cough syrup. Gertrude said her grandmother used to boil it again, after it had been strained, until it was thick and syrupy. Then she put sugar in it and made it very sweet. She would have a full fruit jar of it on hand and would take two spoonfuls whenever she needed it, for hemorrhage. Gertrude did not know what her exact illness was but said she had severe spells of vomiting blood. Ray said he knew of a woman who administered this medicine to her daughter, who had tuberculosis, over a period of several months. The girl eventually became healthy and her mother attributed her improvement to the broomweed medicine.

This plant was also used occasionally to sprinkle water on the heated rocks in the sweat house, according to Ray.

Andropogon

Andropogon gerardii Vitman. Big bluestem.
Plains Apache: *tł'ochiish,* "red grass"; *'áátł'ohe,* "our grass," "native grass."
Bundles of big bluestem or little bluestem (*Schizachyrium scoparium*) grass were used as switches or whips in sweat house rituals. Each man carried in a switch made from a bunch of bluestem grass with the ends trimmed so as to be even, and one end bound up neatly to form a handle. When steam arose from water poured on the hot rocks, each man hit himself about the arms, neck, shoulders, and other parts of the body with his switch. This was supposed to drive away evil, relieve aches and pains, and promote general health. Bunches of sage (*Artemisia ludoviciana*) were used for the same purpose and, in later years, may have been used more often than bluestem (see next entry).

Artemisia

Artemisia ludoviciana Nutt., ssp. *mexicana* (Willd. ex Spreng.) D. D. Keck. White sagebrush, dark-leaved mugwort.
Plains Apache: *tł'éłdíłgyǫǫdee,* "burning stick, easy breaking."
This species of *Artemisia* is a low-growing, herbaceous, aromatic plant with soft, silvery leaves and inconspicuous inflorescence, which the Plains Apache called "sage" in English. Along with mountain cedar (*Juniperus pinchotii*), it was one of the most important plants used in ritual contexts. It was particularly valued, as was mountain cedar, for its distinctive aroma, which was thought to be both aesthetically pleasing and beneficial to health. Sage was used in important rituals such as sweat lodge ceremonies, peyote meetings, and curing sessions. In gathering sage, some stands were known to have a more pleasing odor than others, and these were visited time and again as more material was needed. Fresh sage was preferred for most purposes, but the dried plants were just as fragrant and were used when fresh ones could not be obtained. Fresh sage was often tied in bunches and hung up to dry for winter use.

In a sweat lodge, bunches of sage were laid on the ground around the central rock pit for the participants to sit on. Ray said, "They use sage.

They line it up around the periphery of the lodge and sit on it. It smells fresh when you come out. You can sweat anytime, but it's best when you got a lot of sage, in the spring." Hitting the body with a bunch of sage was supposed to cure sickness.

Sometimes a man used his bunch of sage to sprinkle water on the hot rocks, to produce more steam. The sage or bluestem switches probably also served to remove dirt and grime, aiding the steam and perspiration in cleansing the skin. Fred thought the sweat house was a way of bathing in the old days, and he likened the bundle of sage to a wash cloth. Ray said, "You rub your body with sage while in a lodge. The men sit around and rub dirt off themselves and each other. It gets every part of your body clean. Sage is a deodorant."

Rose said: "They use sage in the sweat lodge. When they pour water on them rocks he hits himself with sage all over. They hit themselves with that sage. You do this anytime, both summer and winter. Some Indians, they still do that when they get sick. You do it anytime that they feel like it, when you're sick, or something like that. Not religious, just like hot springs. It's their way for sickness."

Sage was also used in peyote meetings in much the same way as it was used in sweat lodges. Bunches of sage were laid around the periphery of the tipi and covered with strips of canvas or rugs for people to sit on. (In later years, special quilts, made in long narrow strips, were made by women especially for use in peyote meetings.) Either fresh or dried sage could be used. In addition to this, a bunch of sage was passed around with the peyote staff and gourd (rattle). Each person would take a few leaves, smell them, and rub them over his or her body. Fred described the procedure thus: "In the tipi they take it and wallow it up in their hand and smell it—rub it on them (head and body) and pass it on. Take a pinch of it, maybe two or three leaves, and then pass it on to the next man. Old Indians would rub it on them, pass their hands over themselves and then pass it on. . . . They have a whole bunch of it in the tipi. It sure has a good smell to it."

Ray said the scent of the sage helped counteract the bitterness of the peyote. A person ingesting peyote would try to remember the smell of the sage to keep down nausea.

Sage was also used for medicinal purposes outside of sweat lodge and peyote rituals. It was always carried by doctors and used often in curing ceremonies. Bunches of sage were sometimes hit on aching parts of the body to drive the soreness away. Louise said disease and bad spirits could be taken away by rubbing the body from head to foot with sage leaves, and then throwing them outside. Rose said people used to carry rolled-up sage leaves around with them all the time, to smell whenever they had a headache or did not feel well.

Stems of dried sage were sometimes burned on the skin as a moxa, or counter-irritant, to relieve headache or other pains. In this treatment a thin, sharp-pointed section of stem of sage, about one-fourth to one-half inch long, was inserted into the skin over the hurting area. This stem was then touched with a live coal and allowed to smolder down to the skin. The resulting ember was pinched off or mashed out just as it began to burn the skin. It was not supposed to leave a blister. This treatment was thought to burn the pain away. An alternative method was to light a stem of sage, blow out the flame, and knock the glowing ember onto the skin, letting it die out there. Gertrude had often treated her grandfather for headaches in this fashion, as no other treatment had any effect on him. Concerning this she said, "My grandpa had me do this to him lots of times. He used to get real bad headaches and that's what he wanted me to do—burn sage on him. Sometimes I'd put five or six pieces on him and burn them. I put them up on his forehead sometimes (in region of frontal sinuses) and lots of times he wanted it done back here, behind his ear and on the side of his neck. I'd have to part his hair—he had real long hair—and stick those pieces of stems in there to burn them. He said it helped him."

A plant with grayish appearance and herbaceous leafy stems, hairy goldenaster (*Chrysopsis villosa* [Pursh.] Nutt.), was said to be the "mate" to sage. Several other plants of similar general aspect were also regarded as "look-alikes" to sage, but the elders did not identify these.

Asclepias

Asclepias stenophylla A. Gray. Slimleaf milkweed.
Plains Apache: No term collected.
None of the elders in the study had ever had personal experience with this plant, but Louise had known an old Apache man who collected it

for medicine. She said he used the root, which was long and tuberous, as a chest medicine, but she did not know how he prepared and administered it.

Asclepias tuberosa L. Butterfly milkweed.
Plains Apache: *'ízeełítsowe*, "yellow medicine"; *'it'ąłítsowe,* "yellow flower."
The Apache may have utilized parts of butterfly milkweed for medicine in former times, but the elders were inconsistent in their accounts of its use. Ray thought some part of it was used for stomach medicine, and he had also heard that the root was used as medicine for snakebite. Louise said she knew the Tonkawas used the root to make a fever medicine, but she did not know whether the Apache had ever used it or not.

Bouteloua

Bouteloua curtipendula (Michx.) Torr. Sideoats grama.
Plains Apache: No term collected.
Gertrude identified sideoats grama as the grass used in an operation to remove cataracts from the eye. The flat surfaces of the blades are rough and abrasive, and the edges are thin and sharp. A number of grass blades were picked, washed carefully, and soaked in a basin of water. Then a blade was selected and its roughness tested by looping it up and rubbing it on the arm. The flat, abrasive surface of the looped blade was pulled across the cataract, always in the direction of the inside corner of the eye. This action was done to tear the cataract apart and loosen it from the eye. If necessary, several blades of grass were used for this part of the operation. Then a looped blade was drawn across the eye in such a manner that the sharp edge acted as a scraper, butting and pulling the loosened material away. As Gertrude put it, the cataract was "raked off." Milk from a nursing mother was then dropped in the eye. Gertrude said she had performed this operation for several older relatives.

David Jones (1984: 58) reported that Sanapia, a Comanche medicine woman, used a similar technique for removing cataracts, although he identified the grass she used as *Elymus* sp. (ryegrass).

Cucurbita

Cucurbita foetidissima Kunth. Missouri gourd, stink gourd.
Plains Apache: *daachá'ís'ąąde*, "odor within round object."
The Apache name for this plant referred to the disagreeable odor of the leaves and fruit, which was disliked intensely and likened to the odor of armpits; indeed, Ray said the Apache term could also be used to designate underarm odor. Unless they needed the plant for medicine, the Apache avoided it and admonished their children not to play with it. Connie May was most expressive on this subject: "Yes, that's the one. Better watch it and don't get stink. That thing is sure no good. I hate to smell it. It can't be used for nothing. It's too stink."

Despite its offensive smell, *C. foetidissima* was used for medicinal purposes. Ray reported that the pounded-up leaves, stems, and fruits were an effective remedy for fistula and screwworm infestations in horses. The plant parts were pounded to a juicy pulp and a little water added if necessary. The juice was then poured or swabbed onto the wound, which was bandaged if the horse were gentle enough to permit it. Ray said this medicine would kill screwworms, though it was not considered to be as effective as the juice of ragweed (see entry on *Ambrosia psilostachya* in this chapter).

A decoction prepared from the root of the stink gourd had powerful purgative action and was used to treat vomiting, "bad stomach," constipation, and other troubles where cleaning out the intestinal tract was deemed necessary. Gertrude remembered her father ordering the use of this medicine when her sister had a miscarriage. He said it would clean her out and speed her recovery. The father ordered his son-in-law to dig the root of the stink gourd and told him how to prepare the medicine. This plant had a very long tap root, and apparently the son-in-law came back with most of it because he was complaining about how hard he had to dig to get it all. But just a piece about four or five inches long was used. It was pounded up, put in water, and boiled until the decoction was as dark as coffee. The sick woman drank about half a cup. The father told her if she took the medicine early in the morning, it could clean her out by afternoon. Gertrude said it did work on her sister, both on her bowels and on her uterine tract, and that she suffered no after-pains or other ill effects from the miscarriage. Gertrude gave her sister fever medicine, too, for four days, using a medicine made from the dried leaves of a goldenrod (see entry on *Solidago* later in this chapter).

Cuscuta

Cuscuta sp. Dodder.
Plains Apache: *'ízełítsowe*, "yellow medicine"; *dátsisé'íze*, "some kind of medicine."
Dodder is a leafless, parasitic plant with thread-like yellow or orange stems that sprawl over a host plant. It was an ingredient of the most unusual Apache family medicine found during the research for this study, and the details of its preparation and use exemplify some patterns typical of the use of medicines among the Apache. This medicine belonged to Gertrude, who called it "shingles medicine," or "sore mouth medicine." She possessed the knowledge and the right to prepare it, but the rest of her family could obtain it from her and use it. Gertrude was given the medicine by her grandmother, who had received it from another relative. It was not clear whether Gertrude had ever prepared the medicine alone, but she did at least observe and assist her grandmother in its preparation when she was a girl. At least one of the batches of medicine made by Gertrude's grandmother was reputed to be still in the family. Gertrude gave it to her mother, Rose, who gave it to her oldest son, who presumably still had it, though he had never used it. According to Rose, only an old person could fix this medicine. If a young person prepared it, it would not be effective.

Like "red medicine" (see entry on *Lithospermum* in this chapter), Gertrude's shingles medicine consisted of four ingredients, which were dodder, yellow clay, red ants, and wasps. The dodder was gathered when it was bright orange, carefully cleaned of any bits and pieces of the grass upon which it had twined, rolled into a ball, and dried in the sun. When it was completely dried, it was ready to be pounded with the other ingredients. Yellow clay occurred as a thin layer overlying thicker deposits of white and/or blue clay in the vicinity of natural springs. A suitable quantity of yellow clay was dug in bits from its embankment, molded into a solid lump, and placed on the coals of a hot fire. When the clay was very hard, it was removed and cleaned of ashes and charcoal. It was then ready to use in this medicine or for other purposes. Gertrude said it crumbled easily after it was fired.

The thoroughly dried heads of red ants and wasps completed the list of ingredients. Rose thought two heads of each were needed, but Gertrude said she had used heads of four ants and four wasps. The proportions of dodder and yellow clay are not known, but it is probable that a handful of each were used. All the dried ingredients—dodder, yellow clay, ant heads, and wasp heads—were pounded to a powder on a piece of canvas or cloth. Then the medicine was ready to be stored or used. It would keep indefinitely in its pulverized form.

This medicine was used for a variety of skin ailments—swellings, rashes, blisters, sores, and sore mouth—as well as thrush. Gertrude had helped her grandfather use it when the skin of his arms and upper thorax erupted in an encircling band of red, fluid-filled bumps. Gertrude first cut the afflicted area with a sliver of brown glass, making a number of shallow vertical incisions; then she rubbed the powdered medicine into the cuts. This dried up the eruptions, she said, and stopped the spread of the rash. Another time she witnessed her grandmother use this medicine on a small girl with a mouth so sore and swollen she could not swallow food or water. The old lady broke all the blisters in the child's mouth with her fingers and then swabbed it thoroughly with the powdered medicine. The little girl improved quickly and was able to eat that evening. Gertrude's grandmother had told her that this medicine, and other Indian medicines, had to be applied four times to be effective. Gertrude also said that this and other externally applied medicines were taken on the first and second fingers of the hand and always stroked on with a motion away from the body.

Although the medicine described above was a family medicine, dodder itself was apparently used for medicinal purposes by other members of the tribe. Louise said her aunt dried it, made it into powder, and used it on sores. Ray thought it was used for stomach troubles and menstrual difficulties, but he could supply no details. The Apache term *'izeĺitsowe,* meaning "yellow medicine," was apparently applied to some other medicines as well and did not refer to dodder exclusively. An Apache term for Gertrude's family medicine was not collected.

Dalea

Dalea enneandra Nutt. Nineanther prairie clover.
Plains Apache: *bech'edík'ąąsheh*, "you burn yourself."
Short sections of the straight, brittle stems of prairie clover were burned
on the skin to relieve the pain of headache, rheumatism, and pneumonia
in the same manner as sage stems (see entry on *Artemisia* in this chapter).
Louise preferred prairie clover to sage for this purpose, although she
would use sage when the other could not be obtained.

Echinacea

Echinacea angustifolia DC. Blacksamson echinacea.
Plains Apache: *γoohichíshe'íze*, "tooth-gum medicine"; *'izee'isǫ́ǫ́hee*,
"medicine makes you numb."
   The root of *Echinacea angustifolia* produces a numbing or analgesic
effect on the mouth tissues when chewed, making it useful for relieving
the pain of toothache and sore throat. A little piece of the root was bitten
off, chewed to mix it with saliva, and held against the sore tooth or
gum. Fred thought it was most effective when stuffed into the cavity of
an aching tooth. Ray said a piece of the root could be pounded first and
then held against the sore gum and tooth like a poultice. The sensation
produced by this root was often likened to that produced by Vicks salve
or Mentholatum ointment. Sometimes a piece of the root was chewed
and the juice swallowed to provide a temporary relief for sore throat.
Connie May said it could also be chewed and applied externally to other
parts of the body to alleviate aches and pains. In such cases, she said, the
hurting area would first be cut several times with a sliver of glass; then
the medicine was applied, followed by a hot pack. She had treated her
son for tonsillitis by patting this root on his neck and tying a cloth on.
She also made him chew a piece of the root and swallow the juice.
   This toothache remedy was one of the commonly known medicines
identified in our field study, and probably most people used it before
modern dentistry became available. The roots of this perennial could be
dug at any time of the year but were most easily located in summer,
when the plants were in bloom, or shortly thereafter. A year's supply

was dug then, and the roots were cleaned, dried, and stored for later use. The dried roots were supposed to be more potent than fresh ones, though either could be used.

Eriogonum

Eriogonum longifolium Nutt. Longleaf buckwheat.
Plains Apache: No term collected.
Louise said that her father dug the root of this perennial for medicine, but she did not know what it was used for or what it was called. The root was dug in midsummer, when it was well developed. The dark external covering was discarded, and the reddish inner bark was shaved off in thin layers and boiled like tea. Louise said her father dug enough roots to last all year.

Hierochloe

Hierochloe odorata (L.) P. Beauv. Sweetgrass.
Plains Apache: *tł'o'shįgołchįį*, "grass, it smells."
Sweetgrass was an important ritual plant and was said by the elders to be native to their present territory in Oklahoma, growing at water's edge along small creeks and beside springs. However, botanists have no record of its occurring anywhere in Oklahoma. Gilmore (1977: 14) wrote that sweetgrass could be found in northeastern Nebraska but was more abundant to the north and to the east. Kindscher (1992: 256) essentially agreed with Gilmore's distribution. The Plains Apache probably obtained their sweetgrass through travel or exchange with other tribes living north of them. For many years, dried sweetgrass has been brought into the southern plains area by Americans Indians from outside the state or by commercial traders. At the time of this study it could be purchased in Anadarko stores, both in braided and bulk form. The braids for sale in at least one of these stores came from an Indian reservation in New York state.

According to Connie May, sweetgrass was sometimes used in doctoring, but she could not supply many details on it use for this purpose. She said that only certain doctors had the right to use sweetgrass for curing, and that the sweetgrass used had to be provided by the person being doctored.

A small amount of a braid of sweetgrass would be broken off and put in a fire to produce smoke. The doctor would then smoke the patient, probably using a fan to bring the smoke to various parts of the patient's body. This treatment was supposed to be effective in the treatment of ghost sickness.

Fred said that sweetgrass could also be burned, like cedar, as an incense or fumigant. Presumably the smoke was formerly used in ritual contexts. Other elders could offer no information on its ritual use, though Louise said she knew the Kiowa used it in doctoring practices.

McAllister, who did his fieldwork with the Plains Apache in 1933–34, reported that one Apache man placed some "sweet-smelling grass braided as a small crescent" on live coals to produce smoke when he was doctoring a sick baby. He did this while using a "baby medicine" he had inherited from his stepfather, Daveko (McAllister 1970: 47).

Ipomoea

Ipomoea leptophylla Torr. Bush morning-glory.
Plains Apache: *chiyééyedagółtł'ishii*, "ghost throw it at you"; *tł'ohts'įchizee'íze*, "grass bone medicine."
Bush morning-glory is a bushy, sprawling plant arising from a woody, massive root that can reach over ten feet in length. During our fieldwork in 1963, Dr. Bittle, Louise, and I encountered one of these plants growing at the side of a dirt road where erosion from wind and rain had exposed the huge root. Louise provided us with the Plains Apache name *chiyééyedagółtł'ishii* , meaning "ghost throw it at you." She said the Apache were afraid of this plant because a ghost might throw the roots at them, causing paralysis or some kind of sickness. Paralysis, incidentally, was the main symptom of ghost sickness, a dreaded Apache ailment (Bross 1962: 122).

The root of this plant was probably the bone medicine used by Rose and for which she provided two names, *'isįįts'įįyégołchíshi'*, meaning "I'll knock you down with that," and *tł'ohts'įchizee'íze,* meaning "grass bone medicine." Rose did not identify *I. leptophylla* as the plant used to make bone medicine, but we can surmise the connection as one of her names for her family medicine seems to be a variant of the Apache term given by Louise for bush morning-glory. Furthermore the fact that unusual precautions (described below) had to be taken in using this medicine would tend to support the conclusion that the "bone medicine" root was that of *I. leptophylla*, the "ghost" plant.

Rose's bone medicine was used to relieve the pain accompanying a broken bone or other injury. It would work only for members of her family. A piece of the inner part of the root was chewed, mixed with saliva, and spit out and patted against the injured area, or pressed close with a warm cloth. Rose said the medicine had to be used four times, or once a day for four days. She also said members of the household were supposed to avoid knocking on any object, such as a table, while the medicine was in use or it would not work. For this reason, she said, it was best to use the medicine at night when children were asleep, so as to reduce the chance of someone knocking inadvertently. Rose also hinted that she did not keep the root of this plant in her house at all times but rather gathered it when it was needed, putting up just enough in a buckskin bag to use four times. The extra care taken with this medicine would seem to be directed toward receiving the benefit of the medicine's curative power without attracting a visitation from a ghost.

Gilmore (1977: 58) reported that the Pawnee name of *I. leptophylla* meant "whirlwind medicine," indicating that it was so called because of the twisted and fibrous nature of the gigantic root. Interestingly, the Pawnee also conceived of little whirlwinds (dust devils) as ghosts (Grinnell 1961: 357). The Comanche medicine woman Sanapia stated that whirlwinds or dust devils were visible forms of ghosts (Jones 1984: 65). The Plains Apache were also afraid of dust devils. Gertrude said older Plains Apache always cautioned others not to play with a dust devil—explaining that "it's gonna make you some way [twisted or paralyzed]." She said the old people would always make a cross with their thumb and forefinger to make a dust devil turn away.

Juglans

Juglans sp.
Plains Apache: *chįįshch'įįdą'*, "base of the nose."
The Plains Apache believed that children were especially vulnerable to attacks by ghosts. Whitewolf told Brant (1969: 55) that when he was

little, his mother made him a kind of bracelet to protect him against ghosts. She did this by drilling holes in two dry walnuts and stringing them on a strip of buckskin that she then tied to his wrist. The walnuts used were probably those of *Juglans microcarpa*, which were smaller than those of *J. nigra*.

Juniperus

Juniperus pinchotii Sudw. Pinchot's juniper, redberry juniper, "mountain cedar."
Plains Apache: *gʸad*, no English meaning known; *diłkałéé*, "odor spilling out."
Mountain cedar was one of the most important Plains Apache ritual plants. Its leaves were valued for their pleasing fragrance and used as incense, as a fumigant, and as a ghost repellent.

Specimens of mountain cedar collected in the 1963 field season were identified as *Juniperus virginiana*—erroneously, I believe, because they lacked the cones (berries) that are critical in identifying junipers to the species level. Only very recently, Dr. Wayne Elisens identified mountain cedar as *J. pinchotii*. During a field trip made to a location in eastern Kiowa County, Oklahoma, in June of 2007, he and I and three Plains Apache friends went to a mountain where Plains Apache had for years collected their mountain cedar. Dr. Elisens identified *J. pinchotii* at that time, later confirming the identification in his e-mail message to me of August 23, 2007.

The Plains Apache, like most Oklahomans, refer to all junipers as "cedars." They distinguish two kinds of cedar, "mountain cedar" and "timber cedar," mainly on the basis of a difference in the odor of the leaves. The Apache names *gʸad* and *diłkałéé* were applied to both mountain cedar and timber cedar, although descriptive names such as *gʸadshích'itł'ee*, "kinky cedar," or *gʸadíshjįdée*, "stunted cedar," were occasionally applied to mountain cedar. The Apache term *gʸad* is probably a cognate of the Navajo word for juniper, *kat* (Elmore 1944: 17). One of the names the Plains Apache applied to themselves in the nineteenth century, *gratin*, means "cedar people" (McAllister 1949: 1).

J. pinchotii occurs on dry slopes in the calcareous regions, locally called "slick hills," on the northern flank of the Wichita Mountains. The tree is characteristically short, irregularly shaped, and without a well-defined main trunk. According to Elisens, some *J. virginiana* grow in the same region but at lower elevations, where soils are deeper and there is more moisture. It is possible that some *J. virginiana* from this region could also be included in the Plains Apache category of "mountain cedar."

J. virginiana, the "timber cedar" of the Plains Apache, is ubiquitous in most other localities. It occurs along creeks, in fields, in draws and canyons, and throughout stands of post oak and blackjack oak forest. It is typically tall and symmetrical, with a strong central leader and branches of relatively small diameter. The tall, straight trunks of *J. virginiana* were particularly prized for tipi poles, as described in chapter 5.

The leaves of mountain cedars had an odor that was thought to be sweet and pleasing, especially when they were burned to produce smoke. The dried, crumbled leaves were thrown into a fire or sprinkled on a bed of coals; they made more smoke if they were allowed to smolder instead of blaze. Every family kept a supply of dried cedar leaves stored in a sack or jar. Ray said he crumbled his cedar leaves up fine by pressing them through a screen. Sometimes the leaves were placed in a cast iron skillet along with a live coal. They could also be heated in a skillet over a stove until they began to smoke.

The use of cedar in ritual contexts was connected to deeply rooted beliefs regarding death and the supernatural. One of the fundamental features of Plains Apache eschatology was the belief that the ghosts of deceased persons tended to linger about their former haunts in the hope of perpetrating some harm to surviving friends and relatives (Opler and Bittle 1961: 389). Cedar smoke was one of the principal weapons in the perpetual fight against ghosts: It had the power to repel ghosts and often to counteract their evil deeds because ghosts did not like the smell of cedar, and they would not come near where it was burning. There-fore, tipis or houses were fumigated generously with cedar smoke after the death of a family member. Further, cedar leaves were burned when-ever there was any indication that a ghost might be near, as when a child was sick or crying, when troublesome thoughts of a dead relative could not be put aside, or when a person was ill or depressed. A person seeking the benefits of cedar smoke would reach his or her hands out into the smoke and draw it toward various parts of the body. A doctor using cedar smoke in a healing context might use a fan or a feather to direct the smoke to the patient's body. An older relative might use the hands or a fan to direct smoke to various parts of a child's body.

Cedar leaves were often burned as a precautionary measure, whether or not the presence of a ghost was suspected. Many people burned cedar every day at dusk, carrying the skillet throughout the house so that the smoke would penetrate every room. Fred described the daily use of cedar thus:

> I like the smell of it on the fire. Throw a little pinch of it in the fire and it smells good. You could throw it on a cook stove. It smells good, especially when it's dry. Throw some on the coals in the tipi—smells good. Burn the cedar leaves too, in [the] fireplace, and you can use some in the house if you've got a wood stove. Just sprinkle a little on the fire and it makes the room smell good. Old Indians say it scares spook away, and they say, too, if a child is sleeping in a room alone, if you put some charcoal in a bowl and take it in there and sprinkle a little cedar on it, nothing will bother it. These younger generations wonder what it's for—why you sprinkle that cedar on the fire. They don't know these old Indian ways and they turn up their nose—and laugh—when you sprinkle cedar on the stove.

The scent of cedar was both aesthetically pleasing and emotionally gratifying. It promoted a sense of well-being and a feeling of relief. Louise said, "It gives a happy feeling—good luck. It smells good. They say it keeps evil spirit away." Connie May added, "Take it in all the rooms. Makes the rooms smell good. They say it takes the germs out, when you do smoke the rooms with it. I believe it, cause we use it all time."

Children were protected with cedar smoke on many occasions. When Connie May's husband died, her mother treated Connie May's small children with it, so nothing would bother them. Louise said that a child born mentally or physically defective was treated by a doctor with cedar smoke. It was thought that such a child was impaired because the mother had unknowingly been touched by a ghost at night before giving birth. Had she known of it, she could possibly have prevented injury to the child by using cedar smoke promptly.

The burning of cedar leaves was a traditional part of healing rituals and sweat lodge and peyote ceremonies. A medicine man starting to doctor a patient might smoke a pipe or cigarette first, then burn cedar, and then begin the rest of his treatment. Cedar leaves were thrown on the coals of fires in sweat lodges and peyote meetings. In the latter case, a certain person at each meeting had the responsibility of throwing them on the fire.

Only Louise provided any information of the medicinal use of cedar other than through the smoking ceremony. She had been given a decoction of cedar leaves by a Kiowa woman for hemorrhage and afterpains accompanying childbirth, and she thought it very effective. Neither she nor the other elders had heard of the Plains Apache preparing cedar in this way.

Lespedeza

Lespedeza capitata Michx. Roundhead lespedeza.
Plains Apache: *dóba'ít'ąą*, "coffee leaves"; *kółizhįde'ít'ą'*, "black-water leaves."
This plant has been fully discussed in chapter 3. It was not regarded as a medicine, but "Indian tea" made from its leaves was often prepared for sick people and thought to be beneficial to health. A nursing mother was supposed to be able to build up her supply of milk by drinking lots of Indian tea.

Liatris

Liatris punctata Hook. Dotted blazing star.
Plains Apache: *'izétałjįįbíje'ée*, "crow food."
Rose said that the bulb-like root of *Liatris punctata* was used to treat cuts. The root was probably peeled first and then cut up and pounded. Then it was chewed, and the juice and pulp were spit out on a warm

damp pad and applied to the wound. Gertrude said she had known an old Apache man who used the root for medicine, and she had seen his daughter digging it. She did not know how they used it, however, and did not inquire, since it was one of their family medicines.

Ligusticum

Ligusticum porteri J. M. Coult. & Rose var. *porteri*. Porter's licorice-root, osha.
Plains Apache: *'izeełk'ah*, "medicine fat."
Ligusticum porteri, which in is the Apiaceae or carrot family, is native to high mountain meadows in New Mexico, Colorado, and several other western states, but not to Oklahoma. However, the root of this plant, which the Apache called "medicine fat" in English, has long been highly valued by the Plains Apache as an incense, fumigant, and ghost repellent. All of the Apache elders knew of the medicine fat root and essentially agreed on its appearance and use, but none of them knew which plant the root came from, or what the top of the plant looked like. At the time of this study, Gertrude's family possessed a small amount of this root, which was used in the renewal ceremony for their family medicine bundle every spring, but they did not know how to procure more of it. The plant was identified as *Ligusticum porteri* as recently as June of 2007 in an unusual way:

One of the reviewers of an early manuscript for this book, Dr. Richard Ford, suggested that the medicine fat I described in the section on unidentified medicines might be osha, or *Ligusticum porteri*. With this concrete bit of information I was able to do some research and eventually purchased a pound of whole dried roots from an herb vendor. After smelling the roots, Alfred Chalepah, the ninety-six-year-old son of Rose Chaletsin, agreed that the dried root was indeed the medicine fat known to the Apache elders I had worked with years before. His son, Alonzo Chalepah, age fifty-four and present custodian of family traditions, confirmed the identification at that time, and he confirmed the identification again three weeks later. Thus the answer to a question I had often asked myself—what plant could this medicine fat be?—came belatedly and unexpectedly but, happily, just in time to be included in this publication.

Rose described medicine fat in this way:

Yeah, *'izeełk'ah*, what they put in the fire. It's just like cedar. Way
back, they get it from somewhere up north. They ain't got it around
here. They get it from the north there, in Canada and Montana, and
in them Black Hills. These northern people brings them down. It's
not fat, it's wood. It's a root. The way I see it, it's kind of like rotten
wood. It kind of peels off easy. I don't know the leaf of it. And
these northern people, in the old days they use it, when they didn't
know nothing about this cedar. Then they used that when they was
sick, you know. They use it on anything. Sometimes they use it
when they go to bed, and they use it on their blankets when they go
to bed. They put it on the fire, and smoke it [blanket]. They use it
on their fire. It smells good. We used to have it, but when the old
man [Apache Ben Chaletsin] died, I don't know what happened.
One of his friends gave it to us. It looks greasy, but it's actually not.
It looks like it's damp all the time. It's dark. Some are big ones.
You scrape it, like they do in peyote meeting when they put the
sage in the fire. Scrape off a little and put it in the fire, and smell it.

Connie May, the oldest of the elders, had this perspective:

They call it "fat medicine." It don't grow around here. They get it
somewhere else. It's round, like a ball. It smells sweet. You pinch a
little bit off and put it in the fire and it makes lots of fire [smoke].
Smells good, too. They put it in fire and smoke themselves with it.
It's good for you. Some use it when they're sick. Sometimes when
they feel bad they just smoke themselves. Mostly men use it. I
know I seen them use it in [peyote] meetings—some Kiowas do—
instead of cedar. . . . Yes, old people used it. I don't know where
they get it—they get it from those Northern peoples. Get it from
Cheyennes. I don't think they grow here. . .

It's brown on top but inside it's yellow. I don't know what
kind of plant it is. My folks got some from Cheyenne friends. I
think my mother had some in her medicine bag but we just put it
in her casket.

Louise said: "Medicine fat comes in a round ball—football shape. It's a plant, the root part. It comes from New Mexico. My daddy had some. Some Mescalero friends used to send it to us. My father cut a little off the ball and put it on the coal—fireplace—and smoke come up. It smell good. . . . It seems to me they had medicine fat in the old days, because they got a name for it. I've heard of it a long time."

Finally, Gertrude added: "I don't know where they get it—'izeełk'ah. Apache John [Gertrude's step-grandfather], he burns it, just like cedar. It looks like bark or something to me. It's in a ball and looks like bark. It just breaks off. You can scrape it off. It's got good smelling, too. He used it when he doctors someone. He burned it for us, too—just like cedar."

McAllister, who worked with the Plains Apache in 1933–34, reported that medicine fat was used by the survivors after a relative had died and been buried: "Usually cedar or a root called 'medicine fat' was put on the tipi fire during the first night. 'At nighttime they use some kind of root. They break it up and put it in the fire so nothing bothers them. It is just like you could see the dead. They put this in the fire. You could think of him in your mind.' However cedar and medicine fat were put into the fire at other times, without reference to death. This might be construed as purification rites, or the survivals of such rites, or even as their rudiments, but the old men do not remember anything fixed or compulsory about such conduct" (McAllister 1955: 159–60).

Lithospermum

Lithospermum incisum Lehm. Narrowleaf stoneseed, puccoon.
Plains Apache: *'izełíchihi,* "red medicine."
The roots of *Lithospermum incisum* were used for stomach troubles and to check diarrhea. They were dug when fully matured, after the yellow flowers had dropped off in the early summer. The bark of the root, which was dark red, was considered to be the best part, but it was not thick enough on young plants. After the roots were dug, the tops were pinched off a little below the crown and discarded. The roots were washed and could be dried and stored or used fresh. Dried roots were pounded to prepare them for use as medicine. Fresh roots were simply cut into pieces. Either way, the roots were placed in warm water and let stand to obtain

an infusion that was drunk for various kinds of stomach ailments. Louise said it was particularly good for a child who had diarrhea. The roots could also be prepared by boiling them a short time and setting the decoction aside. When the peelings and other pieces had settled to the bottom, it was ready to drink. Sometimes pieces of root were chewed and the juice swallowed. This medicine had a sweet flavor.

Connie May possessed a family medicine of which *L. incisum* was one of four ingredients. The others were raccoon liver, brown sugar, and a kind of small, aromatic seed that she called "birdseed," which was not otherwise identified. The birdseed used by her mother had been obtained from a Delaware woman, as the plant producing the small seeds did not grow near where Connie May's family lived. These seeds were used mainly as perfume and are discussed more fully in chapter 6 (see section on "Other Perfumes"). The raccoon liver was prepared by roasting it until it was hard and dry. Then it was pounded up fine. To prepare the *L. incisum* root, Connie May said her mother used to shake most, but not quite all, of the dirt and sand off the freshly dug root. Then she pinched the red bark off before it got hard. This bark she pounded on a cowhide till it was soft, and then dried it.

To prepare the medicine she mixed the four ingredients, all of them dried, together. The medicine could be used at once or stored for a long time. It could be used either in powdered form or mixed with water and drunk. It was sweet tasting, and apparently children did not mind putting it into their mouths as a powder and sucking it. Connie May said her mother also used this medicine if a child had a sore mouth, swabbing the powder on the inside of the mouth where it was tender. Her mother also owned a number of other medicines for various ailments, but Connie May never learned about most of them. Connie May thought the ingredients were too hard to find, and the medicines too complicated to fix, so she never bothered with them. When her mother died, most of her medicines were buried with her.

Lophophora

Lophophora williamsii (Lem. ex Salm-Dyck) J. M. Coult. Peyote. Plains Apache: *xosdíszhot'é*, "round sticker."

Peyote is native to south Texas, including the Big Bend region, and to northern parts of the Mexican states of Coahuila and Chihuahua, but not to Oklahoma. However, the Plains Apache obtained this important medicinal and ritual plant through travel, trade, or purchase.

During the peyote ritual, which was held in a tipi and lasted all night, peyote was ingested as a means of achieving a meaningful religious experience. The eating of the peyote was done prayerfully, accompanied by singing, drumming, smoking of corn shuck or oak leaf cigarettes, the burning of much cedar leaf incense (*Juniperus pinchotti*), and the rubbing of crushed sage leaves (*Artemisia ludoviciana*) on the body. There is an extensive literature on the subject of Native American peyotism, and Brant (1950) and Bittle (1954) have fully described the Plains Apache peyote ritual. I will focus here on the information provided by the Apache elders on the manner of collecting, processing, and consuming peyote, as well as their beliefs and attitudes.

Peyote is a spineless cactus. The top of the plant, called the "button," is small, round, and has little tufts of grayish white hair on the ribs. The root, constituting the bulk of the plant, is tapering and succulent, rather like a short, fat carrot. Peyote plants are sometimes hard to spot because they are small and grayish green in color and thus are readily mistaken for the rocks and pebbles among which they grow. The Apache believed it was necessary to smoke a corn shuck cigarette and pray before their eyes would be opened and they could see the peyote.

Apache peyotists and members of their families obtained it from other Indians by sale or trade or by journeying to south Texas, where they either gathered it themselves or bought it from Hispanic collectors who sold the dried buttons. Fred had gathered it himself in the vicinity of Laredo, Texas, and he had also purchased it from a Hispanic dealer there, paying two dollars and fifty cents for five hundred buttons. Connie May described a trip she had made to Laredo with her brother, Fred, and several other Apache several years earlier. When one of the men finally spotted a peyote plant, he did not collect it at once. First, he made a cigarette from Bull Durham tobacco and a cornhusk and lit it. The he handed the cigarette to Connie May because she was the oldest person present. She smoked it and then put it down on the plant. After this ritual, he cut off the peyote button and ate it. After that, they all

found many peyote plants, each person gathering a large sack full. On
this same trip Connie May found a very large peyote plant with a cluster
of many small ones about it. This was apparently a memorable experience for her. She made a prayer right there that the generations of her
family would increase like the young of the big peyote.

In July of 1965 I made a trip to the Laredo, Texas, area with
Gertrude, her niece, Ella Lou Chalepah, and another graduate student in
anthropology. We found the "peyote fields" to be as described above.
Gertrude, being the Apache elder in our group, prayed and smoked a
Bull Durham cigarette before harvesting the first peyote plant. Later we
visited a Hispanic vendor of peyote in Mirando City, Texas, and I was
able to obtain a photograph of the peyote, both dried and green, that he
had for sale.

In gathering peyote, sometimes the tops (buttons) alone were taken,
being sliced off with a knife, and sometimes the whole plant, including
the root, was harvested. The roots were often partly exposed and could
easily be lifted out of the rocky ground. The green plants were brought
back to Oklahoma, where they were washed and the roots cut off. The
buttons were strung on twine and hung up to dry. The roots were
peeled, probably sliced, and dried in the same way.

Peyote could be consumed either fresh or dried, or it could be made
into tea. Dried buttons, which were hard and difficult to chew, were
usually more readily available for meetings than green ones. The Apache
said a person needed to have good teeth to eat dried peyote. Two buttons
were usually taken at a time. Sometimes the dried buttons were pounded
in advance and the shredded pulp was passed around. A small handful
of this was moistened with saliva and rolled into a little ball, which
might then be either chewed or swallowed whole. Sometimes the pulverized buttons were mixed with water and brought to the meeting in a
bottle or fruit jar.

Peyote tea could be made from either the roots or the buttons, but it
was most often made from the roots, with the buttons usually being
reserved for the formal meetings. An infusion of the roots, either fresh or
dried, was prepared by soaking them in water until the liquid became yellow
or brown. Fred said he let his peyote soak in water overnight. Rose made
her tea by boiling the roots a short time, but Louise thought Rose's

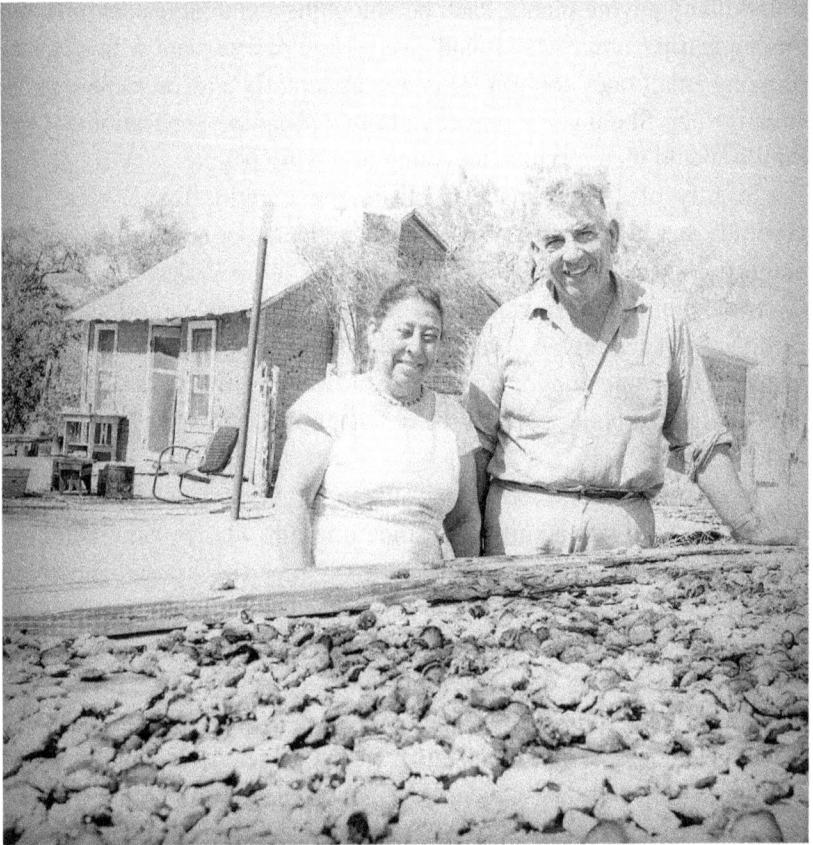

Peyote vendors, Mirando City, Texas, 1965.

method made the tea too strong. Louise said she used seven buttons, pounded, to make her tea. She also let the buttons soak in water overnight to obtain an infusion.

Any way of swallowing down peyote was acceptable and would produce the same results. The effects were believed to be imparted by God through the medium of the peyote plant. These effects could include a heightened perception of colors and sounds, a psychological sense of well-being, a feeling of deep religious experience or revelation, and, perhaps, an alleviation of illness and pain.

In whatever form it was ingested, peyote had a bitter and extremely unpleasant taste. The ingestion of peyote, either as tea or by chewing

Gertrude Chalepah collecting peyote in south Texas, 1965.

the buttons, often produced nausea and vomiting (Bittle 1960: 143–44). This effect was regarded as part of the curative effect of peyote. The vomit contained the bad matter, the material substance causing the physical or mental illness. Regarding this nausea, Connie May said: "Some do [throw up]. It takes all the sickness out. That's a good thing to do. It's their spit; it looks like a soap bubble. When you get rid of that bad stuff, then you're all right."

People handled peyote with great care and consideration, always remembering that it came from God and possessed an intrinsic supernatural power. Connie May said: "They keep it in a safe place. They got to keep its respect." Fred said, in connection with drying the buttons

Gathering peyote in south Texas, July 1965.

outdoors, "You put them on a table or something to dry. If you leave them out on the ground, a dog or something might wet on them." Rose said, "It takes about ten days for them to dry. You got to keep the kids away from it because they handle it and they got dirty hands."

Peyote meetings were often held for the purpose of curing a sick person, who might or might not be present in person. The ingestion of peyote itself, as well as the prayers and actions of the participants, were all believed to have a part in the cure. Peyote was not regarded as a cure-all, but many Apache could tell of a number of near miraculous cures of afflicted persons whom other treatments had failed to help. Peyote was supposed to be particularly effective for flu, fever, colds, pneumonia, arthritis, rheumatism, and mental and emotional disorders.

Lygodesmia

Lygodesmia juncea (Pursh) D. Don ex Hook. Rush skeletonplant.
Plains Apache: *dáábice'íze*, "some kind of medicine."
The stems of the skeletonplant contains a yellow, viscous fluid that in former times was mixed with water and used as eye medicine. One or two drops of this fluid would drop slowly from each freshly cut stem. Louise said the juice from about a dozen stems was mixed with a cup of water; the resulting infusion was then decanted into another vessel before being used in the eye. She said her father and brother had both used this medicine, and that it would get all the pus out of a sore eye.

Matelea

Matelea biflora (Raf.) Woodson. Star milkvine, prairie angle-pod.
Plains Apache: *jédígyashé*, "fruit with bumpy shape"; *'ízełígyahi*, "white medicine."
Louise said that her mother and grandmother used the root of this plant as medicine for chest colds, pneumonia, pain, and swelling. Even though her father was an Indian doctor, he did not use it since it did not properly belong to him. The root was dug according to a certain prescribed way that Louise described: "The way she did, she don't just dig it. She makes a scratch on the ground on the east side, then on the south, then on the west, then on the north side. Then she come back on the east side and commence digging, digging, till she could pull it out. Then she wash the dirt off, clean it. And that vine she just put it back in the hole and cover it all up."

After the root was cleaned, it was kept in a small bag until needed. For use as medicine, a small portion of the dried root was scraped off, chewed until moist, and then applied to the afflicted area. Then a damp cloth was warmed over coals and applied on top of the medicine. Louise said her mother never spit the chewed root out of her mouth forcibly, but removed it gently. She told Louise, "If you blow it out hard the pain gonna come back." The medicine could be applied to the chest to treat pneumonia and colds, or to an aching arm or leg to relieve pain. For internal use, the dried root shavings were chewed and the juice swallowed.

Ray said he had heard of "white medicine" but did not know what plant it came from or how it was used.

Mimosa

Mimosa microphylla Dryand. (= *Schrankia uncinata* Willd.) Littleleaf sensitive-briar, touch-me-not.
Plains Apache: *tł'o'dijiisee*, "grass scratches you."
The Plains Apache used the flowers of *Mimosa microphylla* for a stomach medicine, though the details of their preparation and use could not be obtained. Louise said she used to pick the flowers for her grandmother, who dried them and crumbled them up with another ingredient, making them powder fine. She made the medicine by stirring the powder into water. Louise said her grandmother used it for her stomach, but she did not know in what way. Ray said a solution of the pulverized flowers was drunk for diarrhea and stomach trouble. Rose was inconsistent in her statements regarding this plant. One time she said the flowers were boiled and used to make stomach medicine, but on another occasion she said the plant was not used for medicinal purposes. She may, however, have been mistaken in her identification of one of the specimens.

Morus

Morus rubra L. Red mulberry.
Plains Apache: *'idákxah*, no English meaning known.
Although Bross (1962:115) mentions that a decoction of mulberry roots was taken for stomach trouble, confirmation of this was not obtained during the field work for this study. It is felt that the words "blackberry" and "mulberry" were sometimes confused by elders since the same Apache term was applied to each. Blackberry root (*Rubus* sp.) was used for stomach trouble.

Opuntia

Opuntia macrorhiza Engelm. Twistspine pricklypear.
Plains Apache: *góshchiish*, "red sticker."
The flat succulent stems of prickly pear, which were thought to promote healing, were used by the Plains Apache as a dressing for sores and burns. The thorns were burned off and the pad split in two. The moist, mucilaginous side of one of the sections was applied directly onto the wound and tied securely in place. In case a bullet or arrow had completely pierced an arm or leg, both sections were applied, one on each side of the limb. This treatment was especially apt to be used on wounds suffered while traveling, for prickly pear was common on the dry southern plains, and leaves of the yucca, another common plant of this region, made convenient ties to hold the "bandage" in place. This prickly pear poultice was believed to be an effective remedy for infection, blood poisoning, or festering sores, as it "sucked the poison out." Rose said a fresh application was made every day or two.

Paronychia

Paronychia virginica Spreng. Yellow nailwort.
Plains Apache: *shashgóchináá*, "little 'feist' dog."
Louise said this plant was used in the past as a fan or switch in the sweat house, but she could supply no more details. Presumably it was used in the same manner as bluestem and sage: for hitting the body during the steaming and sweating ritual.

Poliomintha

Poliomintha incana (Torr.) A. Gray. Frosted mint, desert rosemary, "White Sands sage."
Plains Apache: *biládach'íłt'ohéé*, "gray one."
This plant, which in English the Plains Apache elders called "White Sands sage" or "smoking sage," was identified in 1967. The Apache name for the plant and some information on its use had been obtained from Rose in 1963.

The dried, crumbled, aromatic leaves were mixed with tobacco and used in handmade cigarettes. They were smoked often in peyote meetings, where the pleasant aroma was said to counteract the bitter taste of the peyote. Rose described its use: "Jake ordered some kind of sage from White Sands in New Mexico. Irma (a local Indian store owner) gets it and sells it. You can't find this kind in Oklahoma. It's hard to get. Make it fine and put it in a bag. If you're smoking Bull Durham, get a little bit—two or three pinches—and put it in there and it smell good. Tastes good. Better than cigarettes. Nobody ain't got it in the old days—it's hard to get. It's out in White Sands. There's about two or three kinds and you got to find the right kind. You can tell by the smell."

Gertrude said she had watched her grandfather, Captain (Kosope), collect stems of this plant when she was a child. The family had made a visit to the Mescalero Apache Reservation in eastern New Mexico and then went on to the White Sands National Monument area to get the plant. In July of 1967 I went with Gertrude and some members of her family to visit the Mescalero Apache Reservation. When we left Mescalero, we drove to White Sands National Monument, where Gertrude collected a large bunch of leafy stems of *Poliomintha incana* and put them in a paper bag. She said she would later strip off the dried leaves, crumble them up, and store them in a plastic bag or fruit jar. She chewed some of the fresh leaves and used a sprig of the plant to hit herself on her elbow and wrist joints, presumably to relieve aching. She said she always tried to keep a supply of the dried leaves on hand.

P. incana resembles *Artemisia ludoviciana* (which the Apache call "sage") in having soft, silvery, pubescent leaves and a pronounced pungent odor, but it is actually in the family Lamiaceae rather than the family Asteraceae, to which *Artemisia* belongs.

Proboscidea

Proboscidea louisianica (Mill.) Thell. Ram's horn, unicorn plant, common devil's claw.
Plains Apache: *gǫ́ǫ́chełabedízhishé*, "horn"; *'ishjánabishéézhyąą*, "old lady's toenail."

Gertrude Chalepah collecting *Poliomintha incana* at White Sands National Monument, New Mexico, 1967.

The seeds of this plant were eaten by a nursing mother to build up her supply of milk. When a woman had a baby her relatives might hunt for the crescent-shaped pods and bring them to her so she could eat the seeds.

Quercus

Quercus marilandica Münchh. Blackjack oak.
Plains Apache: *sǫch'ił*, "star brush, oak."
Quercus muehlenbergii Engelm. Chinkapin oak.

Louise Saddleblanket selecting blackjack oak leaves for use as cigarette papers, 1964.

Plains Apache: *sǫch'iłíbaahi*, "white oak."
The Plains Apache used the leaves of these oaks as cigarette papers, wrapping them around a suitable mixture of tobacco. Of the two species, blackjack oak leaves were preferred for this purpose. They were thought to have a finer flavor, whereas the leaves of the chinkapin oak were reputed to make the mouth sore or itchy if many cigarettes were smoked. Blackjack leaves were thicker and rougher than chinkapin leaves. Although blackjack leaves were preferred, elders said they would smoke either kind, depending on what they could get.

The use of oak leaves for cigarettes seemed to be associated primarily with the rituals of the Native American Church and was probably intro-

duced to the Plains Apache with the peyote religion. It was felt that all
cigarettes smoked during peyote meetings should be rolled with either oak
leaves or corn shucks. According to Weston La Barre (1964: 38), the use
of ceremonial cigarettes by the Plains tribes had its origin in Mexico and
the Southwest. Both the Mescalero Apache and the Lipan Apache used
oak leaf cigarettes in their peyote rituals (La Barre 1964: 41).

Ideally, oak leaves for cigarettes were gathered in early summer or
midsummer, when they had attained their full size but before they were
damaged by insects, wind, or disease. The carefully selected leaves were
dried between the pages of a book to keep them flat. When needed for cigarette papers, they were soaked in water for a short time and the excess
moisture blotted away. In the past they were softened with saliva. Louise
said she had seen old men put the dried leaves on their tongues to moisten
them. Before drying, the leaves were trimmed into square or oblong shapes
with scissors. Formerly, they were either trimmed with a knife or the
uneven edges were bitten off with the teeth. Ray said old people used to
make their leaves into oblongs by biting them as they were telling stories.
The leaves remained green in color even after they were dried.

Fred said that when he prepared to go to a peyote meeting he soaked
fifteen or twenty of the dried, trimmed leaves in a bowl of water for five or
ten minutes. Then he drained and blotted them and put them in a billfold.
They stayed damp throughout the night, retaining enough flexibility to
roll into cigarettes. He used Bull Durham tobacco for the cigarettes.
Louise said that cigarettes rolled with oak leaf "papers" could be smoked
anytime, and not only in a meeting or ritual context. Both men and women
smoked. Some men preferred pipes for casual smoking, but others liked
blackjack oak or cornshuck cigarettes.

Rhus

Rhus glabra L. Smooth sumac, shumate.
Plains Apache: *'ikáshchįįde*, "mix with something."
Sumac leaves were mixed with Granger Twist or some other suitable
chunk tobacco and smoked. They were gathered in the fall when they
had turned scarlet. Louise said that she and her mother used to spread a
blanket underneath the sumac bushes and strip the leaves off onto it.

The leaves were set out in the sun for a day, and then, partially dried, they were greased with tallow and placed in the sun again. The grease was worked in carefully, so that each leaf was coated. When thoroughly dried, after about two or three days, they were sacked up and stored until needed. Louise said she and her mother used to prepare about three large flour sacks full for her father to use throughout the year. The sacks were hung up on the wall so worms would not get into the leaves.

The smoking mixture was prepared in relatively small quantities by the man who would use it and kept in his smoking pouch. Two or three handfuls of the cured sumac leaves were cut up fine and mixed with a quantity of cut up Granger Twist or other tobacco. Louise said her father used to cut up the sumac on a cloth-covered board held in his lap. When he had prepared enough, he put it aside and cut the tobacco, shaving it in narrow slices from the chunk. Then he mixed the sumac and tobacco together, rolling and crumbling the mixture until it was soft and homogeneous. He tested it by smoking a pipe full. If it did not have the flavor he liked, he added more sumac or more tobacco until it was right. A greater proportion of sumac than tobacco was used. Louise's father smoked his mixture in a small pipe that had a stone bowl. The father of Connie May and Fred also used a pipe for smoking this blend. Fred said he did not think anybody smoked sumac anymore—it was too much trouble to fix.

Rubus

Rubus sp. Blackberry.
Plains Apache: *'idákxah*, no English meaning known.
The Plains Apache used a decoction of blackberry root for diarrhea and stomach ache. The root was dug in summer and could be used either fresh or dried. Ray said the medicine was very bitter, causing the mouth to pucker. Regarding its effects he said, "If you got irritation in your bowels caused by eating fresh fruits and meat, it draws your stomach and the poison just runs."

Sapindus

Sapindus saponaria L. var. *drummondii* (Hook & Arn.) L. D. Benson. Western soapberry.

Plains Apache: *chishłítsowe*, "yellow wood"; *má'abíje'e*, "sheep food"; *má'abíchąą*, "sheep feces."

Ray said soapberry bark was used for constipation, kidney trouble, and to start the flow of menstrual blood. Bark was obtained from green sticks of about one to two inches in diameter. Limbs of this size had smooth bark. Shavings of the bark were boiled for about fifteen or twenty minutes, until the resulting decoction was reddish or brown in color. The liquid was then strained. A cupful of the medicine was taken three or four times a day. Ray said it would flush out the kidneys and start menstruation. It could thus be used to induce an abortion. He said it was also taken by men who had gonorrhea.

Schizachyrium

Schizachyrium scoparium (Michx.) Nash var. *scoparium* (= *Andropogon scoparius* Michx.). Little bluestem.

Plains Apache: *tł'ochiish,* "red grass"; *'áátł'ohe,* "our grass," "native grass."

Little bluestem was used for sweat lodge switches in the same way as big bluestem, as described above under *Andropogon.*

Solidago

Solidago sp. Goldenrod.

Plains Apache: *tsízekáshé'íze,* "cold and fever medicine" (term from Bross 1962: 64).

Fred picked a specimen of *Solidago* and identified it as a fever medicine belonging to his family, but it could not be keyed to the species level because a flowering specimen could not be obtained. It grew in dense shade along a shallow, dry creek bed. Fred said he had obtained his fever medicine from a certain spot west of Broxton, Oklahoma, for years. Before that he had gathered it along the Washita River west of Fort Cobb.

Fred said his father had received knowledge of this medicine in a dream wherein an old friend came to him, told him what plant to procure, how to fix the medicine, and what to use it for. The medicine was used, possibly for the first time, to treat Fred's brother-in-law, who had been sick with a high fever for several days. The sick man took a decoction prepared from the fresh green leaves, and shortly after the first dose, the fever broke.

It is very likely that this first and dramatic success plus its supernatural revelation was largely responsible for the great faith that Fred and his family had in the efficacy of this medicine. Both Fred and his sister, Connie May, were enthusiastic about its power to cure fever, and other elders also spoke of it with respect. Louise, the sister of Fred's brother-in-law, said, "I believe in that medicine. It's good." However, Louise claimed she did not know what plant was used, and she felt that it would not work for her if she did. She said: "Connie May has got good fever medicine and I don't know nothing about that. Fred might know, and his children, but me, I don't know nothing about it. It goes with his peoples. . . . When Connie May goes down to look for it she take her grandchildren or great-grandchildren and probably they know it. But I don't know it. No, I never asked about it. There's no use—they won't tell. I think it's wrong for me to ask."

Fred and Connie May said this medicine could be found along creeks and rivers. They described the plant as having reddish, leafy, nonbranched stems; their father had specified that they look for a plant with red stems. They said this plant never had flowers. Interestingly enough, Fred, whose vision was failing due to glaucoma, once produced some branches of a plant with red stems and simple linear leaves that he said were those of his fever medicine. This specimen proved to be a species of *Salix* (willow). Later, he corrected himself, saying the *Salix* specimen was not the right plant, and he identified the *Solidago* picked from the Broxton area as the real fever medicine.

To prepare the leaves, a number of leafy stems were picked at one time, tied in a bunch, and hung up to dry. Then the leaves were stripped off the stems and folded into a cloth, which was then squeezed to crumble them. The crumbled leaves were stored in a bag of cloth or buckskin until needed. To make the medicine, a decoction was prepared from fresh or dried leaves. Fred said four pinches of the leaves were dropped into a pan of boiling water and boiled or steeped until the liquid was yellow or dark brown in color. It was then strained and drunk warm, not hot. Bross

(1962: 71) quotes Connie May as saying she always threw the leftover leaves out in the grass, the idea being that "you throw the sickness away with that medicine." He further states that she spoke to the medicine, instructing it to cure the patient.

This medicine and its mode of preparation and use was very similar to a fever medicine that Gertrude had obtained from her grandfather. Gertrude's medicinal plant, *Teucrium canadense* (see next entry), also grew in dry woods beside creeks and had reddish stems and an inconspicuous inflorescence.

Teucrium

Teucrium canadense L. Canada germander.
Plains Apache: *tsísdeekáshé'íze*, "fever medicine."
The dried, crumbled leaves of this plant were used to prepare a decoction for treating fever or ailments in which fever might occur. Information concerning this medicine came entirely from Gertrude, who learned the medicine from a grandfather. She said it was good for abdominal pains accompanying diarrhea, menstrual cramps, and the afterpains of childbirth and miscarriage.

This medicine was prepared and used in almost exactly the same way as Fred's fever medicine (see *Solidago*, above). In making the medicine, Gertrude said she always took a pinch of the powdered leaves between her thumb and forefinger, dropping it into a pan of boiling water with her hand describing a cross. She dropped in four pinches in this manner, and then let the medicine steep until it became brown, like tea. She said it had a pleasant aroma and did not taste bitter. She did not strain the liquid but rather let the leaves settle to the bottom of the pan and decanted the rest into another vessel. After the medicine was taken internally, the leftover liquid was poured on the hands and rubbed on the stomach where the pain was. Or the medicine might be spit into the cupped hands and then patted on the sore place. This was supposed to help the pain go away. Any leftover medicine and the leaves were thrown out on the ground in a spot where no one would be likely to walk on them. This action is reminiscent of Connie May throwing out the leftover leaves of her fever medicine (see *Solidago*) into the grass. It would seem that this kind of behavior is indicative of an underlying conviction among the Apache that the medicines possessed intrinsic power apart from the ministrations of the curer. Because it possessed power, it was to be treated with respect, just as peyote plants were handled carefully and guarded from casual contact with humans and animals.

It is possible that Gertrude occasionally used another plant, in addition to *T. canadense,* in preparing her medicine, though they were the same to her. Like Fred and Connie May, she looked for her medicine in the shade of trees along creek banks, and she described it as a leafy, herbaceous plant with single, nonbranched stems that were red at the base. She said: "The stem is red. And sometimes it's got square stem and sometimes it's got maroon colored stem that's not square. You kinda find it in a bunch, like that Indian perfume, and the stems don't have any little branches on them. Just got one stem and leaves.

Typha

Typha sp. Cattail.
Plains Apache: *k'aazół,* no English meaning known.
Rose said that cattail pollen was used to make a cranky, jealous child good-natured and happy. For example, a woman expecting a new baby might hire someone to perform a ceremony over an older child who was inclined to be jealous. The pollen was rubbed on the child four times, and his forehead and cheeks were painted. She said her father always gathered two or three cattail heads when they were mature, so he would have them on hand. He used the pollen on his son's children. Rose called this plant *tł'oogááh,* meaning "top of the grass."

FUNGI USED FOR MEDICINAL PURPOSES

Fungi are no longer considered to be members of the plant kingdom but are treated as a separate kingdom. The Plains Apache elders mentioned at least two different types of fungi used for medicinal purposes, and I am presenting their information here, although I cannot specify the species of puffball(s) or even a higher level classificatory group for the bracket fungi.

Lycoperdon

Lycoperdon spp. Puffball.
Plains Apache: *nobíízįįs*, "earth, its wart"; *dazhé'abiɣéétsi* and *zázaɣą́ą́bigɣeetsį́*, both terms meaning "coyote penis."
The Plains Apache used the dry powdery material on the inside of old puffballs as a styptic to treat skin ailments—sores, wounds, and poison ivy. Young puffballs are white and firm all the way through, but as they mature the exterior turns dark and the spores inside appear as a yellowish-brown or greenish-brown powder. This powder was rubbed into raw sores or wounds and was supposed to dry them up. Gertrude said her grandmother used to gather puffballs whenever she encountered them and tie them in a rag to save. Connie May did not think they could be saved, but she said they could be found anytime they were needed. Louise said puffballs appeared on the ground after thunder and lightning.

Bracket Fungi

Scientific term cannot be specified.
Plains Apache: *ko'ébi'jɑɣíi*, "wood ear."
Louise said her father gathered a kind of bracket fungi from blackjack oak trees, dried it, and kept it in a sack. When he needed it, he crumbled it up into powder and applied it to bad sores.

UNIDENTIFIED RITUAL OR MEDICINAL PLANTS

The Plains Apache no doubt formerly knew and used many other wild plants for medicinal purposes. Two plant medicines that were discussed but not positively identified during the study are described here, and possible identifications are suggested. An aquatic plant used in a rain-producing ritual is also included.

Pain and Swelling Medicine

Rose's family used the root of a certain plant to make a pain and swelling medicine. Gertrude described it as a vine-like or prostrate plant growing on prairie hillsides and bearing, in the fall, a yellow fruit the size and shape of a plum. She also said that it had little pink flowers. She tried to find a specimen of this plant for me but was unsuccessful. However, she said her brother still dug it occasionally for their family. The dried root could be stored indefinitely. To use it, a piece was bitten off and chewed, then spit out on the fingers and applied to the swollen or hurting area. Gertrude said that when this or other Indian medicine was applied externally, it was always rubbed on with a movement away from the body, never rubbed upward, or back and forth. For mumps or a sore throat, juice from the chewed root was both swallowed and applied externally. Rose and her brother still used this medicine for the pain of broken bones or aching joints.

Gertrude said that this medicine was given to her family by Apache John. Rose said: "It was that old man [Apache John] that gave us this medicine. He gave us those sticks and he showed us what kinds of roots he's got. He called it that wild plum, in the ground. I guess you seen that plant. It's got little cherries, like, on it. They are red. In the ground, there is the root. It's real hard to get. It grows in the mountains. He said that he learned it from one old man who had that root." Rose also said that Apache John used the medicine to treat snakebite.

The description of the plant suggests that it might be *Astragalus crassicarpus* Nutt., groundplum milkvetch, which is native to Oklahoma and other Great Plains states.

Sneezeweed and Sneezing Medicine

Another medicinal plant known and described by all the elders but never identified from a plant specimen was "sneezeweed," which the Plains Apache called *begǫnįda'íkashee*, "it makes you sneeze." A medicine consisting of sneezeweed alone or sneezeweed in combination with other ingredients was called *nída'íkazhe'ízeh*, "sneezing medicine." In the field, Ray identified as sneezeweed a specimen of *Thelesperma filifolium* (Hook.) A. Gray var. *intermedium* (Rydb.) Shinners, or stiff greenthread, but other elders would not confirm the identification because the flower heads did not produce sneezing when they were sniffed. They all admitted that it resembled sneezeweed in that it had many small, yellow flowers.

Several species of *Helenium* are also commonly called sneeze-weed. Gustav G. Carlson and Volney H. Jones (1940: 532) reported that the Comanche used smallhead sneezeweed (*Helenium microcephalum* DC.) to induce sneezing for clearing the nasal passages and to expel afterbirth. David Jones (1984: 57) identified the sneezeweed used by a Comanche medicine woman to induce violent sneezing as *H. micro-cephalum*. Unfortunately, no specimens of *H. microcephalum* were collected during the field seasons of 1963 and 1964, so its identification as the sneezeweed of the Plains Apache is tentative. The elders did, however, agree that sneezeweed grew in or at the edge of shallow ponds, buffalo wallows, or any kind of depression where rain water collected. Gertrude and Rose also said the plant grew in ponds near prairie dog towns. All of these habitats are typical for *H. microcephalum*.

The dried, crumbled flower heads of sneezeweed plants possessed the quality of inducing uncontrollable sneezing when inhaled. Even a slight whiff was supposed to produce a fit of sneezing so violent that it caused the nose to run and cleared the nasal and sinus passages. Because of this property, the sneezeweed flower heads were saved and snuffed to relieve headache and the congestion of head colds. Ray also said they were inhaled when a person felt drowsy and wanted to wake up, because a fit of sneezing would apparently get rid of the sleepy feeling.

Sneezeweeds were also a favorite medium for teasing one's joking relations, those with whom one had a joking relationship, especially the young and naïve. Connie May narrated the following anecdote: "One time my grandpa was smashing some (sneezeweed flower heads). He took just a little bit on his fingers and said to my brother and cousin, 'You boys want to smell some good perfume?' He put some on their nose and oh, they started sneezing. They sneeze and sneeze, and snot and stuff [was] running out their nose. He sure was laughing aloud. My grandma was laughing too. . . . She say, 'get outside,' and she took a bucket of water out there and pour it on their head and make them blow. Finally they got all right." Fred also related how his cousin once tricked him into smelling some sneezeweeds, again under pretext of smelling perfume.

Other plants native to the Great Plains have the property of inducing sneezing when inhaled, especially in dried or powdered form. Gilmore (1977: 80–81) says the pulverized leaves and tops of *Boebera papposa*

(= *Dyssodia papposa* (Vent.) Hitchc.) were snuffed up the nostrils by the Omaha to relieve headache, and that the Teton Dakota reported that this plant was always found around prairie dog towns. Gilmore also reports (1977: 38) that the pulverized bark of the root of *Gymnocladus dioicus*, Kentucky coffeetree, as well as the pulverized, dried pods, causes uncontrollable sneezing. Although both of these plants occur in Oklahoma, none of the elders ever mentioned their use for any medicinal purpose.

Sneezing medicine was a dry powder that when inhaled, produced the sneezing fits thought to be beneficial for several ailments. Depending upon who prepared it, it may have consisted of the dried crumbled heads of sneezeweed flowers only, or of the pulverized heads in combination with other ingredients. It may, in fact, have contained any plant materials that would induce sneezing. Connie May said her grandfather's sneezing medicine contained sneezeweed and other ingredients. She remembered her father gathering sneezeweed in a buffalo wallow west of Mountain View in Kiowa County. He put a handkerchief over his nose while he broke off the stems. Then he wrapped them up in a sheet so they would not bother anyone in the wagon. Louise's father, a medicine man, also had a sneezing medicine, but she did not know what was in it, as she had only seen it as a powder tied up in a piece of canvas and stored in his medicine bag. Sneezing medicine was used to treat headache, colds, and pneumonia. It was also given to a person who had a caved-in chest as a result of broken ribs or a dislocated shoulder. It was hoped that, when the person sneezed, the bones of the rib cage would pop back into place.

Water moss

Plains Apache: *dlaah*, no English meaning known.
According to Rose, the fronds of an aquatic plant, locally called "water moss" in English, were used long ago in a ritual to make rain. A medicine man (shaman) would take some from the water, make some kind of motions, squeeze it, and throw it back into the water. This ceremony was supposed to produce rain.

CHAPTER 5

Material Culture and Firewood

Like other bison-hunting Plains Indian tribes, the Plains Apache were heavily dependent upon animal products for manufacturing items of material culture. Tipi covers were made of bison hides. Clothing was cut from animal skins and sewn with sinew. Containers for storage and transport were made of rawhide or tanned skins sewn into bags and pouches. Many tools and weapons had component parts of bone, hide, sinew or gut, joined with glue obtained by boiling hooves. Ties and lashing materials were made mostly from strips of rawhide, as were ropes and bridles. Animal products—feathers, claws, teeth, small animal and bird pelts, dew claws, and hair—were often used for decoration and adornment. There was no basketry, nor was any kind of textile or plant cordage manufacture recalled by any elder in the study. However, plant materials were indispensable for many purposes.

PLANTS USED IN MATERIAL CULTURE

Aesculus

Aesculus glabra Willd. var. *arguta* (Buckley) B. L. Rob. Ohio buckeye, Texas buckeye.
Plains Apache: No term collected.
This buckeye, which is native to western Oklahoma, is a shrubby species, rarely reaching the height of a small tree. Plains Apache children played with the hard, black seeds, sometimes stringing them together to make beads or belts.

Ambrosia

Ambrosia trifida L. var. *texana* Scheele. Texan great ragweed, giant
ragweed, "bloodweed."
Plains Apache: *-biɣagólałíchihíi*, "it makes your hand red."
The Plains Apache elders all referred to giant ragweed as "bloodweed."
The plants are common in the region's waste places and creek bottoms.
These shallow-rooted annuals make a rank growth and reach a height of
twelve to fifteen feet by the end of summer. The main stalks are straight
and tough, becoming hard and stiff when they dry up. Bloodweed stalks
were the preferred material for making winter windbreaks around tents or
tipis. In a land where winds are frequent and often powerful, the protection
of windbreaks added a considerable degree of comfort to winter life. They
were often erected around tipis in the old days whenever the winter camp
was a more or less permanent location, and they were still built frequently
from 1900 to 1920, when many activities were still conducted in tents.

The windbreak of bloodweed stalks was set up against a framework
of upright posts and horizontal willow poles, placed a few feet away from
the tent. The upright poles were cut from blackjack oak, post oak, or other
suitable trees. Sturdy posts were set in the ground at the four corners of the
area to be enclosed. Slender willow poles were fastened horizontally to
the upright posts at heights of three and six feet above the ground. An
opening was left on the east side through which people could pass in and
out. Then a shallow trench was dug at the base of the framework, and the
bloodweed stalks, roots down, were set in the trench. They were placed
close together, so thick that they screened the tent from view and stopped
the force of the wind. The leaves were left on, as they added to the screen.
The bloodweed stalks were lashed to the horizontal poles, and then the
trench was filled in and the dirt tamped down firmly on both sides. Thus
stabilized, the windbreak would last a long time, affording effective protection from the strong northerly gusts of winter. Connie May said the
windbreak also provided privacy for the family and discouraged passersby
from making off with any belongings. Sunflower stalks were sometimes
used along with bloodweed in making windbreaks. Sometimes sunflowers
alone were used, and occasionally willow was also utilized, but the favorite
screening material was bloodweed.

The mature bloodweed plants could also be used to thatch an arbor, according to Fred. Bunches of bloodweed were attached to the arbor frame, root ends up, in overlapping layers, like shingles on a house. Louise said bloodweed stalks were sometimes used by children to make toy tipi poles.

Amphiachyris

Amphiachyris dracunculoides (DC.) Nutt. (= *Gutierrezia dracunculoides* (DC.) S. F. Blake). Prairie broomweed.
Plains Apache: *bekózhǫǫshe*, "broom"; *tł'o'xéhach'i'a'*, "grass, burns quick."
The branches of mature broomweed were almost bare except for the small, yellow flowers and terminal leaves. Brooms to sweep our the tipi or tent were made from two or three mature plants tied into tight bunches.

Andropogon

Andropogon gerardii Vitman. Big bluestem.
Plains Apache: *tł'ochiish*, "red grass"; *'áátl'ohe*, "our grass, native grass."
The following discussion applies also to little bluestem (*Schizachyrium scoparium*), as these two important prairie grasses were used in the same way.
   The Plains Apache elders called the big and little bluestem grasses by the same two terms. These tall, native bunch grasses are two of the most important plants on the prairie, little bluestem predominating on the uplands and in the open areas of blackjack oak–post oak woods, and big bluestem favoring the deeper soils of bottomlands and well-watered draws. Both take on a reddish hue after frost. The bluestems were useful in a number of ways, one of the most important being their utilization for mattresses in tipis or tents. For a mattress, a canvas was spread on the ground, and bunches of dried bluestem were cut with a knife and arranged on the canvas to the desired thickness. Then another canvas was placed on top of the grass, and the whole bed was secured in place by pegs driven into the ground. Sometimes one large canvas would be used to hold the grass stuffing. Bunches of grass were placed on one

half of the canvas and then the other half was folded over them and tacked in place with heavy thread or twine. In former times, animal pelts were laid over the thick layers of grass, but later, quilts and blankets were used as bedding. Bluestem pallets lasted several months, after which time they got soft and crumbly and had to be replaced. One advantage of this kind of mattress was that in wet weather, a person could simply reach under the bed and take out a handful of dry grass to start up the morning fire.

Bunches of dry bluestem were also used to make brooms for sweeping out the tipi. This grass was also used occasionally, instead of willow branches, as arbor thatch. Bunches of bluestem were lashed to the horizontal poles of the arbor frame in overlapping rows. They made a thick shade.

The Apache term *'áátl'ohe*, meaning "our grass," reflects the fact that the bluestem grasses, especially little bluestem, which had a much wider distribution than big bluestem, were both abundant and very significant in Apache culture. They were nutritious and palatable grasses for horses and other livestock. The bluestems were also used as a sweat lodge switches, as discussed in chapter 4.

Artemisia

Artemisia filifolia Torr. Sand sagebrush, silvery wormwood.
Plains Apache: *tł'éłdisgóódedíchaahí*, "big sage."
This plant grows in the western part of the present Plain Apache territory. Its feathery, gray green branches are very soft and were sometimes used as a substitute for toilet paper. Branches of this plant were used occasionally as padding material for pallets or beds. The Plains Apache term for this plant, *tł'éłdisgóódedíchaahí*, was also applied to one or more of the sagebrushes that grow in the Rocky Mountain area.

Baptisia

Baptisia bracteata Muhl. ex Elliot var. leucophaea (Nutt.) Kartesz & Gandhi. Longbract wild indigo, plains wild indigo.

Plains Apache: *tł'o'íɣał*, "grass rattle"; *'ichíshcheełbishagǫ́'ǫhee*, "turtle shade" or "turtle arbor"

This species of *Baptisia* has stout, upright stems with large, elongated racemes (flower clusters) protruding laterally from the stems. The elders reported that box turtles often sheltered themselves from the summer sun under this prairie "turtle arbor." When persons wanted to find box turtles (which the Plains Apache often ate), they would look for them in the shade of this plant.

The mature seed pods are black and, containing several hard, loose seeds, make a rattling sound when touched. Ray said that the sound was very much like that of a rattlesnake. Both Ray and Rose said the dry seed pods could be use as rattles. Rose said the pods were wrapped in a rag and given to babies to play with.

The dried seed pods of other species of *Baptisia* were also used as baby rattles.

Carya

Carya illinoinensis (Wangenh.) K. Koch. Pecan.
Plains Apache: *ch'iłxạshé*, "put it in your mouth, crack it."
The Plains Apache used pecan wood for making items such as walking canes, hoe handles, tent pegs, and the like. However, the wood was thought to rot quickly, and it was therefore not much liked for tent pegs or as support posts for arbor structures. Western soapberry and post oak were preferred for these purposes. Connie May remembered watching her father make a bow out of pecan wood for her little brother. Rose said the wood could be used to make game sticks.

Celtis

Celtis laevigata Willd. Sugarberry, hackberry.
Plains Apache: *tsédíłł'itséé*, "hard seed."
Hackberry wood was not much utilized for making artifacts, though Fred thought it would make good tool handles if it were properly seasoned. He said it would warp if used green.

Cornus

Cornus drummondii C. A. Mey. Roughleaf dogwood.
Plains Apache: *k'áhkạs*, "arrow branch."
This species of dogwood is common in the region, growing along creeks and streams in the shade of larger trees. The wood was used for a number of purposes, perhaps the most important being the manufacture of arrow shafts, which were always made from dogwood. Its special suitability for arrow shafts consisted, at least partly, in a characteristic of its growth: the lower portion of a young dogwood shoot was often straight and unbranched for a length of from two to three feet. These shoots were thus ideal for the making of arrow shafts. The bark was easily removed, and the absence of side branches facilitated smoothing and shaping. In making arrows, shoots of about one-half inch in diameter were cut, the bark removed, and the shaft scraped to the desired thickness. While green, the shaft could be easily straightened by holding it at the mid-section with the teeth and bending the ends into the proper alignment with the hands. In the old days only men made arrows.

Straight, peeled dogwood sticks were also strung together to make backrests, which were hung at the head of beds in tipis. Larger sections of dogwood were used for making other items, such as walking sticks and bows. Dogwood bows were suitable for children's use or for shooting small game, but they were not strong enough for killing buffalo and other large animals. Heavy-duty bows were almost invariably made of bois d'arc. Drumsticks were also made from dogwood on occasion.

Equisetum

Equisetum hyemale L. Scouringrush horsetail, common scouringrush.
Plains Apache: *koyátł'oh*, "water grass"; *k'azółbe'éésidé*, "resembles cattail."
Whistles were made by children from short sections of the hollow stems (internodes) of this plant. A piece about one and one-half inches long was cut, flattened out, and blown. Louise had heard that a person blowing these whistles was calling for snakes, which were supposed to like the

sound produced. This plant grew about the edges of creeks and swampy places, localities that the Apache feared were inhabited by snakes.

Fraxinus

Fraxinus sp. Ash.
Plains Apache: *ch'iłdíłgyǫǫts'ee*, "wood splits easy."
The Plains Apache sometimes used the wood of ash for making bows, but they considered it to be inferior to bois d'arc for this purpose. It may have been used, when convenient, to make other wooden articles.

Gaura

Gaura coccinea Nutt. ex Pursh. Scarlet beeblossom, scarlet gaura.
Plains Apache: *k'á'zhayee*, "little arrow."
The straight, rigid stems of the mature plant were used to make arrows for children to shoot from their small bows. Ray said that his grandfather used this plant to make toy arrows for him, fitting the tips with spines from prickly pear, and made him practice shooting at grasshoppers until he could hit them at a distance of about ten feet. Ray said he would tire of trying to hit grasshoppers with his arrows and would start catching them with his hands to show the old man. His grandfather was not fooled, however; he made Ray go back and practice shooting again until he could hit the mark. *Dalea enneandra* Nutt., a plant with similar bare, straight stems, though smaller and more brittle, was regarded as the "mate" to the little arrow plant (see entry on *Dalea* in chapter 4).

Gymnocladus

Gymnocladus dioicus (L.) K. Koch. Kentucky coffeetree.
Plains Apache: *jįįsha*, no English meaning known; *séétą́níbíchish*, "stick game tree."
The wood of the Kentucky coffeetree was a favorite material for making scoring sticks for the woman's stick game. A pastime of older women, the stick game was played by moving certain pieces around a cloth

"board" or "map." At each turn, the number of places moved depended upon the score obtained by a throw of four stick-dice onto the center of the board. These stick-dice were made from ten-inch sections of small branches split in half longitudinally, with a stripe down the center of the inside surface. Three were painted red, and one blue. Kentucky coffeetree branches were ideal for making the stick-dice because they contained a pithy inner chamber of dull red color. Branch sections of the desired length were cut and allowed to season before being split lengthwise and smoothed. The reddish inner chamber formed a natural red stripe down the center. The blue stick still had to be painted, of course.

The fruit of this tree is a pod containing hard, black seeds about three-fourths of an inch to one inch across. Louise had once seen a Cheyenne woman collecting a sackful of these seeds to use as poker chips. Each player was to buy one dollar and fifty cents worth of "chips," each one being worth five cents in the game.

Helianthus

Helianthus sp. Sunflower.
Plains Apache: *datízhił*, no English meaning known.
The Plains Apache occasionally used tall sunflower stalks in making windbreaks, either in combination with bloodweed stalks (see entry on *Ambrosia* in this chapter) or alone. Their manner of use was the same as that for bloodweed, being placed against a frame of willow poles in a trench with dirt mounded up against their base to stabilize them. Otherwise, sunflowers were thought to have an unpleasant odor and were usually avoided. None of the elders reported that the seeds were eaten.

Juglans

Juglans microcarpa Berl. var. *microcarpa* (= *Juglans rupestris* Engelm.).
Little walnut, western black walnut.
Juglans nigra L. Black walnut.
Plains Apache: *chı́ı́shch'ı́ı́dą*, "base of the nose."
The chocolate brown heartwood of both species of black walnut was straight-grained, hard, and durable, and it took on a mellow luster with

age and much handling. It was used for the manufacture of a number of items, especially articles that were to be enhanced with decorative carving. Among objects made from walnut were pipe stems, skewers for securing tipi openings, drumsticks, and walking sticks. Wooden bowls were also made of this wood, and fence posts were sometimes made from walnut trees of the right size. In making a pipe stem, a suitable piece of the heart-wood was shaped and the bore laboriously burned out with a piece of red-hot wire. Drumsticks were preferably made from walnut, though other materials were also used. They were often decorated with ornamental carving. Drumsticks used in Native American Church ceremonies at the time of this study were usually carved of seasoned walnut heartwood.

Louise said that small whole walnuts, presumably those of *J. micro-carpa*, were sometimes perforated and strung to make children's bracelets or beads. These were supposed to keep the children fat. The elders in our study had never heard of the Apache using walnut husks to prepare any kind of dye, although Louise knew a Kiowa man who dyed his gray hair black by rinsing it in a bucket of water in which walnut husks had been soaked for several days.

Rose said that walnut leaves could be mixed with white clay to make a green pigment. Speaking of white clay, she said, "They mix it with leaves. White clay and walnut leaves makes green. Sometimes it comes out dark green. Make green color by boiling walnuts in water." It is not clear whether she meant boiling walnut leaves or walnut husks.

The small nuts of *J. microcarpa* were sometimes also used as bosses in tying the buckskin drumhead onto the iron kettle water drum used in peyote ceremonies.

Juniperus

Juniperus virginiana L. Eastern redcedar, "timber cedar."
Plains Apache: *gyad*, no English meaning known; *diłkałéé*, "odor spilling out."
Tipi poles were almost always made of cedar, which was hard, strong, and resistant to rot. For this purpose, tall, straight trees with small side branches were selected and cut; men performed this task, although women were often on hand to specify the kind of poles they wanted.

The side limbs were cut off, and the poles were dragged back to camp. The poles were so heavy that only two or three at a time could be pulled by a horse. They were tied to a wooden saddle with rawhide ropes, the large ends up and the small ends dragging the ground—they were supposed to be easier to pull this way. Back at camp, the bark was removed at once with a draw knife, or if this job could be postponed, the poles were rolled in a fire as this was thought to make the bark come off more easily. Louise said that in the past, a tool made of a stone knife inserted into a wooden handle about eight inches long was used to remove the bark. It was held with one hand on the handle and the other on the stone blade. The large ends of the poles were then sharpened so they could be set in the ground. After the poles were prepared, they were allowed to dry out at least two weeks before being used. Tipi poles, thus prepared, were said to last many years. If the lower end became dull or broke off, it was resharpened and used again; this process was repeated until the pole became too short to be of service.

Although species of pine suitable for tipi poles were not native to the Plains Apache territory in Oklahoma, the Apache knew that some kinds of pine were used by other tribes for tipi poles. However, they much preferred cedar for this purpose, saying it was stronger and more long-lasting than pine. Connie May said her family used to get tipi poles from trees growing in a small canyon a few miles west of Fort Cobb. Louise said many Indian people obtained their poles in the vicinity of Mount Sheridan in the Wichita Mountains.

The wood of eastern redcedar was important for other purposes in addition to making tipi poles. It was a favorite material for fence posts because of its long-lasting, rot-resisting properties. The reddish heart-wood was attractive in color and grain, strong, and easy to carve. It was used for items such as drumsticks, tipi skewers, and staffs. Rose said peyote staffs could be made from cedar. Ray reported that flutes were made from the red heartwood: The length of wood used for the flute was split in half lengthwise and a semicircular trough was gouged down the center of each half, one end remaining intact. Holes were drilled in one of the halves. The pieces were then fitted together, tied with buckskin in four places, and secured with glue made from red gum

Plains Apache erecting framework for tipi, using poles of *Juniperus virginiana*, 1967.

(*Silphium laciniatum*, see entry in chapter 3). The hollowed-out troughs formed the bore of the flute, the bottom end being left solid.

Maclura

Maclura pomifera (Raf.) C. K. Schneid. Osage orange, bois d'arc.
Plains Apache: *kǫ'éɫítsowe*, "yellow wood."
Bois d'arc was originally native to eastern Oklahoma and parts of adjacent states but has long been naturalized throughout the state. It has been widely

planted for hedges, fences, and shelterbelts in western Oklahoma. The elders of this study regarded bois d'arc as an indigenous tree. So far as they knew, it had always been popular for the manufacture of a number of artifacts, particularly bows. Gilmore (1977: 24) said the Missouri River tribes regarded bois d'arc so highly that they obtained it from Oklahoma, whenever possible, for making bows.

Bois d'arc wood was especially prized for making bows because it is hard, tough, and strong. Beside it, all other woods were considered inferior. Ray explained, "Bois d'arc is outstanding. Some bows, like ash, may break when you are going to kill the buffalo or facing the enemy. They are too brittle. But bois d'arc will stand by you. You can't break that."

Bows were made from the heartwood, which was bright orange in the green wood but turned an attractive yellowish brown with age. Green wood was used so that it could be bent into the proper shape. A suitable length of wood was scraped to the desired thickness and left wider in the middle, with the ends tapered somewhat. The midsection of the bow (the grip) was supposed to be the thickest part, but not too thick. Rose expressed it this way: "A man who knows how to make bows makes a good one. When some men don't know how, they make dummy ones. Sometimes your bow got a big belly. If it's got a big belly, it won't shoot straight."

The arc was created by bracing the bow against the knees and pulling the ends forward with the hands. If the bow was too thick to bend, it was scraped some more on the inside. This scraping and bending process was repeated until the bow was considered to be of the right shape and degree of stiffness. Then the ends were notched and a bowstring of twisted sinew fibers was attached and drawn tight enough to hold the bow in an arc. The bow was allowed to season in this position, after which it retained a permanent curve.

Other objects reported to be made from this wood were war clubs, drumsticks, pipe tamps, peyote staffs, fence posts, and cradle boards, and presumably this list could be expanded to include many more items. Ray said the notched war clubs, or ceremonial "whips," were made either of bois d'arc or mulberry because these woods were heavy.

Gertrude remembered seeing some drumsticks of bois d'arc that had been given to the Apache by the Pawnee when she was a little girl. The end of each stick was decorated with a carving of a human head. Louise said her father used a bois d'arc pipe tamp to press the tobacco down or clean out the bowl of his little peace pipe. It was about the thickness of a pencil, pointed on one end, and stored in his pipe bag. She said her father made it of bois d'arc because this wood did not burn fast. Sometimes pipe tamps were decorated with ornamental carving.

Mentzelia

Mentzelia nuda (Pursh) Torr. & A. Gray var. *stricta* (Osterh.) Harrington.
Bractless blazingstar, bractless mentzelia.
Plains Apache: *'ít'ą'édiłtł'įshé*, "leaves stick to you."
The leaves of this plant were rough and would cling to any surface upon which they were placed. They were played with by children, who pasted them on their clothes for "decoration." Sometimes the leaves were unknowingly slipped onto the dress or blanket of a relative with whom one had a joking relationship, so that people could get a laugh at his or her expense.

Morus

Morus rubra L. Red mulberry.
Plains Apache: *'idákxah*, no English meaning known.
Mulberry wood was sometimes used for making bows, but it was not as hard and tough as bois d'arc. Bows made from mulberry were usually used for target practice or light hunting. For heavy-duty bows, bois d'arc was preferred. Mulberry wood was used to make a number of other items, including war clubs, tool handles, and fence posts.

Paronychia

Paronychia virginica Spreng. Yellow nailwort.
Plains Apache: *shashgóchináá*, "little 'feist' dog."

Connie May said two or three bunches of this plant could be tied together at the base and used as a broom to sweep out the tipi. She said her grandparents used it this way.

Phytolacca

Phytolacca americana L. American pokeweed.
Plains Apache: *k'áábehíbéshee*, "to color the arrow."
Poke berries are about the size of small grapes—soft and very juicy. The Plains Apache used the juice of the dark blue fruits as a stain to decorate arrows, bows, and war clubs. Several of the ripe fruits were crushed, and the design was applied to the item either with the finger or with a stick dipped in the juice. The resulting color was permanent and of a dark reddish hue. Sometimes the juice was mixed with white or yellow clay to get certain shades of color.

Arrows were marked both for identification and for decoration. The kind of design applied depended upon the individual's taste. Fred said he painted his arrows red (with red paint stone) so they would be easy to find when he shot them off. Rose described the use of poke berries thus: "Each man has a special mark on his own arrow. When they kill enemy and maybe he get hit with two or three arrows, they will know whose arrow belongs to who. They mark them with a plant. They got them grapes like fruit. . . . Take one off and mash it with hand and put it in a cloth. Use a blunt stick, soak stick in it and mark arrow from feather down. Some got rainbow design. Others decorate between feathers. That all they use. Looks like striped candy. It's pretty. They don't ever decorate whole shaft of arrow."

A set of arrows made by an old Apache man, still living in 1964, was on display in an Anadarko store. These had designs painted on the wooden points at the bottom of the arrow, but apparently any decoration on the lower part of the shaft was unusual. Louise said only the upper part of the shaft was marked.

Bows, if colored at all, were usually stained all over instead of being marked with designs. Feathers were dyed by boiling them with poke berry juice, probably diluted with water. War clubs might also be decorated with designs that were drawn on with poke berry juice. Other pigments used in decorating artifacts were obtained from red paint stone, yellow clay, white clay, and charcoal.

Pinus

Pinus sp.
Plains Apache: *neezch'į'*, no English meaning known.
Tall, slender pine trees suitable for tipi poles were not native to western Oklahoma, but in former days, the Plains Apache occasionally made tipi poles of pine. The Plains Apache in Oklahoma preferred eastern redcedar (*Juniperus virginiana*, see entry in this chapter) for this purpose, as it was supposed to be more durable and have greater strength than pine. Furthermore, cedars suitable for tipi poles were readily available in Oklahoma.

Plantago

Plantago sp. Plantain.
Plains Apache: *'izátł'o'łįbenidáákashe*, "some kind of grass, horse racing." At least two species of plantain, *Plantago patagonica* Jacq. (= *P. purshii* Roem. & Schult.) and *P. wrightiana* Decne., figured in a game called "horse racing" that was played by Plains Apache boys. Both of these plantains had leafless, slender spikes of small, graying or purplish flowers that, while immature, were downy or silky to the touch. The game, or race, consisted of trying to find the longest plantain spike in a certain length of time. When a group of boys decided to play this game, bets were made first, and then the boys scattered to look for long stems. After a time the leader called everyone back. The boy who had picked the longest stem won the "horse race" and collected the bets.

Populus

Populus deltoides Bartram ex Marsh. Eastern cottonwood.
Plains Apache: *'inįįlįį*, no English meaning known.
The cottonwood was apparently little used by the Plains Apache for any purpose. Even as firewood it was a poor choice because it burned away quickly, leaving no coals. But Rose said that a branch of cottonwood

was used occasionally as a fan, to brush the flies away. Temporary replacements for broken tipi poles were cut from cottonwood, but these were used only until new cedar poles could be obtained. Connie May said she was afraid of cottonwood trees because they were brittle and she had heard of branches breaking off during strong winds and falling on tents. Cottonwood bark and small branches were mixed with acorns and fed to horses to keep them fat during a severe winter.

Psoralidium

Psoralidium tenuiflorum (Pursh) Rydb. (= *Psoralea tenuiflora* Pursh). Slimflower scurfpea.
Plains Apache: No term collected.
The father of Louise had told her that a section of the lower stem of this plant could be used as a scoop for removing marrow from animal long bones. He had used it this way when he and some companions were out hunting buffalo. They would cut off a leg bone and crack it open, using the scoop to get at the fresh marrow. On another occasion, Louise commented that the old Apache never went after the marrow with a sharp-pointed implement, such as a knife.

Vestal and Schultes (1939: 75) mentioned that the Kiowa used the stout stems of this plant as a fork when cooking and eating buffalo meat.

Quercus

Quercus macrocarpa Michx. Bur oak.
Plains Apache: *sǫch'ił*, "star brush"; *sǫch'iłíbaahi*, "white star brush."
Quercus marilandica Müench. Blackjack oak.
Plains Apache: *sǫch'ił*.
Quercus muehlenbergii Engelm. Chinkapin oak.
Plains Apache: *sǫch'ił*, "star brush"; *sǫch'iłíbaahi*, "white star brush."
Quercus shumardii Buckley. Shumard's oak.
Plains Apache: *sǫch'ił*.
Quercus stellata Wangehn. Post oak.
Plains Apache: *sǫch'ił*, "star brush"; *sǫch'iłích'itł'e*, "curly star brush."

Several species of oak are native to the Apache territory in Oklahoma. Blackjack oak and post oak are the dominant species of the Cross Timbers forest, occurring on the dry, thin-soiled, sandy uplands. Shumard's oak and bur oak grow along creek and river bottoms and in well-watered, deep-soiled places. Chinkapin oak (*Q. muehlenbergii*) grows in many localities, often interspersed in stands of blackjack oak–post oak timber.

The Plains Apache term *sǫch'ił* was applied to all oaks, but when used alone, it usually referred to blackjack oak. The term was also used to refer to any stand of scrubby brush or timber, which in this country inevitably contained a large number of blackjacks. Other species of oaks could be distinguished by descriptive terms such as those given above for bur oak, chinkapin oak, and post oak.

The Plains Apache utilized all species of oak for fence posts and other items of material culture. Post oak, being very abundant, was the usual choice for fence posts. Blackjack oak was also used occasionally for fence posts but was not as long-lasting as posts make from other oaks. The bark was usually left on the wood used for fence posts.

Most often, the Plains Apache used post oak timbers in constructing the basic supporting frame of brush arbors (see the discussion of brush arbors in the entry on *Salix* in this chapter). For the upright posts they cut straight-trunked trees of about six to eight inches in diameter at the base of the trunk and with a good fork about nine to ten feet above ground. The posts were set two to three feet deep in the ground, and the dirt was tamped around them firmly with a thick stick or a crowbar. Ridgepoles, also made of straight, stout trees, were laid across the forks. The ridgepoles could be any suitable length so long as they did not sag. A framework of willow poles was added to the basic structure of uprights and ridge poles and thatched with willow branches. Other suitable trees, such as elm and soapberry, could also be used as arbor supports, but oak was abundant in most localities and was most often used.

The Plains Apache also used oak for other structures, such as meat drying racks and tripods. It was used on occasion for tent poles, to hold out the sides of conventional wall-type tents, and for tent pegs, though soapberry (*Sapindus saponaria*, see entry in this chapter) was preferred for these purposes. The bark was removed from poles used for racks and tent poles.

Other items were no doubt also made from the white oaks, including post oak. Ray said oak was good for making hand drums because it was sturdy. For this purpose a section from a hollow tree of suitable diameter was sometimes used, or advantage was taken of a piece of a trunk or limb with a large knot that could be pushed out easily. In former times wooden bowls for eating utensils were made from white oak. The charcoal formed from burning oak firewood was supposed to be best for making the black pigment used in painting designs on artifacts.

Quincula

Quincula lobata (Torr.) Raf. (= *Physalis lobata* Torr.). Chinese lantern, purple ground cherry.
Plains Apache: No term collected.
The mature seed pods of this plant consist of a bladdery calyx enclosing a capsule of seeds. Children played with these pods, popping them in their hands or stepping on them.

Robinia

Robinia pseudoacacia L. Black locust.
Plains Apache: *kǫ'ébigɣoskǫ́ǫ́lįhii*, "wood, its thorns."
Black locust, native to eastern Oklahoma, had become fairly common in shelterbelt and woodlot plantings in Plains Apache territory by the time of our study. It was used for fence posts and for fuel. Ray said it made longer-lasting fence posts than elm.

Salix

Salix nigra Marsh. Black willow.
Plains Apache: *-bitsístł'ąąɣąą*, no English meaning known.
Salix interior Rowlee. Sandbar willow.
Plains Apache: *k'ásts'ǫǫts'ee*, "drooping limbs."
The Apache elders recognized two kinds of willow, corresponding to the two species listed here, both of which are represented by specimens in the plant collection. Other species may also be native to this part of

Oklahoma, and each would fall into one of the two Apache categories, depending on their size and appearance. The willow called *-bitsístł'ąąyąą* (*Salix nigra*) was a large tree with a short, thick trunk and many branches jutting out at all angles from a low crown. The Apache term could not be analyzed during the study, but it apparently referred to the dark colored, deeply corrugated bark on the trunks of the large trees. The Plains Apache regarded this willow as practically useless, except for shade. All other willows fell into the category of *kásts'ǫǫts'ee*, the "drooping limbed" willow (*S. interior*). Some of these were tall and slender, with few side branches; others were short and bushy. Finer distinctions among willows could be made when necessary by employing descriptive terms such as "willow with flat wide leaves," "willow with narrow leaves," "willow with dark trunk," and other such phrases. Willows of the *kásts'ǫǫts'ee* category were extremely useful in several contexts, including for the construction of brush arbors and sweat lodges.

Brush arbors were important structures of living during the typically uncomfortably hot, dry months of summer and early fall. Arbors were often constructed next to the tipi or house. The tipi entrance faced east, and the arbor was always placed on the east side of the tipi so that persons could pass back and forth from tipi to arbor with ease. The arbor was left open along its north side. Much of the daily activity in summer was conducted in the shade of the arbor, and members of the family often slept there on hot nights. Arbors were also erected as temporary shelters when families camped together at dances or on special occasions. They were still being built in the mid 1960s, although canvas tarpaulins were replacing them for providing shade for cooking and eating areas at tribal powwows. Brush arbors were cooler than canvas, for they permitted the air to circulate freely and did not trap hot air.

Essentially, arbors consisted of a thatched, lattice-like framework of willow poles supported by a basic frame of stout upright posts and ridgepoles. The uprights were straight trunks of suitable trees such as post oak (see entry on *Quercus* in this chapter) or elm, with a Y-shaped fork at the upper end. For a small arbor, two or three uprights were set firmly in the ground in a row, and a ridgepole or poles were laid across them through the forks. Slender willow poles about twelve to fourteen feet tall were set shallowly in the ground, about six feet out on each side from the uprights and about two or three feet apart. The tops of these were pulled down and tied to the ridgepole, the upper half of the willow pole being made to bow outward in the shape of an arc so as to provide the maximum space within. Conventionally, the north side of the arbor was left open, and the back side, or south end, was rounded out with the willow pole framework. When the vertical poles were all in place, similar willow poles were lashed onto them horizontally, at about two foot intervals, beginning about three feet from the ground. Formerly, all the poles were stripped of their bark, which was then used for lashing the frame together. However, baling wire and rope have long since replaced bark ties. When the framework of poles was complete, bundles of leafy willow switches were used to thatch the arbor. Each bundle, consisting of several switches four to five feet long, was woven in and out of the horizontal poles, the cut ends up and the leafy tips hanging downward. Bundles of willow were thus attached to the whole frame in overlapping layers until the entire arbor was covered. The thatch extended almost to the ground on all sides except the north, providing thick and effective shade during all times of the day. Sometimes small openings were left on other sides for convenience in entering or leaving. A smaller arbor to shade the cooking area was sometimes added to the main arbor at the northeast corner.

A larger arbor could be constructed by enlarging the basic supporting structure to two or more rows of uprights, the posts of each row being connected by ridgepoles passed through their forks with stringers connecting the posts of different rows. Willow poles were then laid horizontally across the roof, paralleling the stringers, and were lashed to the ridgepoles. The resulting flat roof was thatched like the sides. Proportionately more materials were required for the rest of the arbor.

Willow poles were also used in the construction of sweat lodges, which are discussed in some detail in chapter 4 under the heading "Sweat Lodges."

In former times, the Plains Apache used strips of willow bark as lashing material for many purposes. Louise said her mother used to peel the bark from a green tree and keep it moist in a bucket of water. Then it was still pliable when she needed it to tie something. Once dry, the bark became brittle and could not be used again. Willow limbs were

Plains Apache willow-thatched brush arbor at annual Manatidie dance encampment, 1961.

also used occasionally in making windbreaks, being lashed to a supporting structure in the same manner as bloodweeds (*Ambrosia trifida*, see entry in this chapter).

The Plains Apache also used willow for several other purposes. Long ago a kind of hat or turban made from flexible willow twigs was worn during daytime dances or ceremonies as protection against the sun. Backrests were made from peeled willow sticks of about a finger's thickness and cut to uniform length. The green sticks were straightened in the same manner as arrow shafts, perforated at the ends, and strung together with sinew or cord. Sometimes the sticks used for backrests were decorated by staining them some color. Backrests were suspended from a forked stick at the head of the bed. They were long enough so that the lower end folded under the bed and was held in place by the weight of the person sitting on it. Willow withes were also used to make the framework of the canopy shading an infant's cradle board. They were peeled, and the bark was used to tie the frame together. It was covered with cloth or hide to shelter the baby.

Sapindus

Sapindus saponaria L. var. *drummondii* (Hook. & Arn.) L. D. Benson. Western soapberry.
Plains Apache: *chishłítsowe*, "yellow wood"; *má'abíje'e*, "sheep food"; *má'abíchąą*, "sheep feces."
Soapberry wood was heavy, strong, and close-grained, with a yellowish cast. The Plains Apache used it for many purposes, but it was especially esteemed for making tent poles and tent pegs.

The use of tipis declined after allotment in 1901, and more and more the Apache came to use the rectangular wall tents of canvas sold by white merchants. The sides of these tents were secured to vertical poles, about two to three inches in diameter and about six feet long, set in the ground outside the tent. To make these poles, straight, young soapberry trees of proper diameter were cut, the side branches were removed, and the bark was shaved off with a metal draw knife. When seasoned, the poles would last indefinitely. Pegs for tacking down the lower edges of tents or tipis were also made of soapberry when it was available.

The Plains Apache used soapberry for many other purposes. It was suitable for fence posts, and also for the uprights and ridgepoles of arbors. Meat drying racks and tripods were often made of stout soapberry sticks with the bark removed. Bows and tool handles were also made from this wood. Louise had used it for the handle of an awl she had made. The point of the awl was made from an old parasol frame, which she said was the best metal for this purpose.

The black, shiny seeds of the soapberry, about one-half to three-fourths of an inch in diameter, were used as playthings by children.

Boys played marbles with them. Sometimes they were perforated and strung as necklaces or bracelets for children.

The Apache term for soapberry fruits meaning "sheep food," *má'abíje'e*, is probably a euphemism for *má'abí chąą*, the term meaning "sheep feces." Louise said soapberries were called by the latter term because "when sheep goes restroom, it be in little balls." This term was not supposed to be used in the presence of relatives with whom one had a relationship of respect, in which case the polite term, *má'abíje'e*, was employed.

Schizachyrium

Schizachyrium scoparium (Michx.) Nash var. *scoparium* (= *Andropogon scoparius* Michx.). Little bluestem.
Plains Apache: *tł'ochiish*, "red grass"; *'áátl'ohe*, "our grass, native grass."
Little bluestem is included in the discussion in this chapter of *Andropogon gerardii*.

Solanum

Solanum dimidiatum Raf. Western horsenettle.
Plains Apache: *boh*, "top," "spinning object."
This plant with many stickers was a nuisance to brush into, but the underripe fruits, resembling small, green tomatoes, were made into tops for children to play with. The largest ones with the most nearly spherical shape were picked for this purpose. A stick about three inches long and the diameter of a matchstick was whittled out, sharpened at one end, and inserted through the core of the hard fruit so that the pointed end protruded about one-fourth to one-half inch from the bottom. The upper part of the stick constituted the handle. An area for spinning the tops was delimited by a circle drawn in the ground with a stick, and a smooth surface was prepared by clearing away dirt and obstructions. Sometimes a heavy piece of canvas or a piece of rawhide was laid down. The top was set in motion by rotating the handle back and forth briskly

between the hands, the fingers held straight out and thumbs pointed up, and dropping it on the prepared surface. A symmetrical top, skillfully released, would spin a moment or two before slowing down, wobbling, or traveling into some object. Top-spinning contests were often held among children, and sometimes wagers were made on the outcomes. In former times, boys used to bet arrows. A good top was supposed to spin rapidly without deviating from the vertical or traveling very far horizontally. Such a top was said to have "gone to sleep," and the top that "slept" the longest won the contest for its owner. The fruits of *Solanum elaeagnifolium* Cav. (silverleaf nightshade) and *S. carolinense* L. (Carolina horsenettle) could also be used for tops, but they were not so large. Rose considered *S. elaeagnifolium* to be the "mate" to the real "top" plant because it resembled the latter closely but was smaller and had fewer stickers.

Sorghum

Sorghum halepense (L.) Pers. Johnsongrass.
Plains Apache: No term collected.
An introduced plant, Johnsongrass quickly became established in Oklahoma, and because of its aggressive spreading habit, it soon became common in fields and pastures and along roadsides. In general, the Plains Apache disliked Johnsongrass because it was a "white man's plant," but they found to be of use in some ways. As it was tall like bluestem, it could be used for the same purposes (see entry on *Andropogon* in this chapter). It was sometimes tied in bunches and used to make brooms to sweep out the tent, or laid down in thick layers for pallets or mattresses.

Ulmus

Ulmus americana L. American elm, white elm.
Plains Apache: *chiłjíí,* "black wood."
Ulmus rubra Muhl. Slippery elm, red elm.
Plains Apache: *chiłjíí,* "black wood."
No clear-cut Plains Apache term for elm or a variety of elm was obtained in our study, though one may have existed. The term *chiłjíí* was applied to both species of native elms as well as to other trees with dark, scaly bark,

such as the Kentucky coffeetree (*Gymnocladus dioicus*), black locust (*Robinia pseudoacacia*), and occasionally even the large willow (*Salix nigra*), which was also called -*bitsístł'ąąγąą*. However, in English, at least, elders made a distinction between "red elm" (slippery elm) and "white elm" (American elm); imported species, such as Chinese elm, were included with white elm. A distinguishing feature of the red elm was its large leaves, which when full size, were rough and scratchy like sandpaper.

The Plains Apache used the tough, strong, and heavy elm wood in a number of ways. Red elm was the preferred wood for making saddle trees. The wood selected for the saddle tree would be a section with a suitably shaped fork, with one end of the fork being shaped into the pommel; the other, the cantle. Louise said that when the saddle tree was carved out, a tanned buffalo hide was sewn over it. Ray said the saddle tree was covered with wet rawhide, which shrank to fit the contours tightly as it dried.

Red elm was also good material for fence posts. According to Ray, red elm was easy to split, white elm having a twisted grain and being therefore much harder to work with. However, white elm was also used on occasion for fence posts, and both elms could be used as supporting posts for brush arbors. Bows were occasionally made from elm, though bois d'arc was preferred for this purpose. The inner bark of red elm was sometimes stripped off in fairly long lengths and used as ties or lashings in the same manner as willow bark.

Elm trees, especially white elms, were valued for the shade they provided in summer. Though the Apache seem never to have planted shade trees, they appreciated those trees that by chance shaded parts of their yards, living areas, or dance grounds. An arbor was not necessary if a good shade tree was at hand. The broad, spreading crowns of white elms, drooping almost to the ground at the edges, cast a deep and cool shade throughout the day.

Vernonia

Vernonia baldwinii Torr. Baldwin's ironweed.
Plains Apache: *tl'o'łįį'ádadach'íł'įįshíí*, "grass you make horse out of"; *łįįbéétsaséé*, "whip."

This tall herbaceous plant bearing attractive clusters of purple flowers in late summer was common in dry pastures. It grew in clumps comprised of a number of long, tough, leafy stems. These stems were used as a "hobbyhorse" by Plains Apache children in their play. A long stem was cut, and all the leaves except those at the very top were stripped off. The remaining tassel of leaves was the "head" and the bare stem was the "body" of the stick horse. The elders in our study gave slightly varying names for this plant; however, all of the names given were descriptive of the way in which the plant was used as a toy horse. Since ironweed stems were so tough, they were also utilized on occasion as improvised quirts to prod on a lazy horse. Connie May said people also cut bunches of it to made beds of, because it was soft. Sometimes ironweed and sage branches were used together to make pallets that were covered with hides or quilts.

Another plant, *Verbena stricta* Vent. forma *stricta*, was called the "mate" to the hobbyhorse plant; it resembled the latter very superficially in having tall, leafy stems topped by a purple inflorescence. It also came into flower at approximately the same time. Actually, these two plants come from different botanical families, the Verbenaceae and the Asteraceae, respectively, and differ considerably in morphological characteristics. The fact that such dissimilar plants were regarded as member of the same plant pair may reflect the relatively slight importance of both in Apache culture.

Vitis

Vitis spp. Grape.
Plains Apache: *dáłts'ał*, "hanging in bunches."
Woody sections of grape vine could be worked into a number of useful objects while green; dried grape wood was difficult to work with. In using this material for any purpose, the Plains Apache used the natural shape of the vine, often twisted into right angles and U-shaped curves, to their advantage.

Connie May said saddles were occasionally made of grape wood, though she offered no details on the manner of their construction. According to Rose, wooden stirrups were made of grape wood. Presumably, suitably curved sections were utilized for this purpose. (However, the Plains Apache did not often use stirrups, which sometimes consisted merely of loops of rawhide slung from the saddle tree.) A section of grape wood with an approximate right-angle bend was used to make the handle for a hide fleshing tool. Such an implement probably approximated the size and shape of fleshing tools made from elk horn. A serrated metal blade was attached to the shortest segment of the wood, and the long part served as the handle. Fred said that his grandfather used a length of grape wood with a natural crook at one end to make a ceremonial staff. He brought the grape wood back to camp and carved it, sitting on a blanket or piece of canvas, praying all the while he worked. The staff was used in the Manatidie, the Blackfeet Dance.

Yucca

Yucca glauca Nutt. Soapweed yucca, "Indian cabbage."
Plains Apache: *dayígya*, "appears whitish."
Yucca leaves, which are narrow and have tough fibers running through them longitudinally, were used by the Plains Apache as ties when other materials were not readily available. For example, if a man was wounded while out hunting or on a raid, a poultice might be applied to the injury and tied in place with strips of yucca leaves. Hairbrushes were also made from the stiff, sharp-pointed leaves. Connie May had often watched her grandfather make yucca brushes. He first cut leaves of uniform length. The base ends were then folded over and bound tightly, forming the handle and leaving the stiff, pointed tips for the bristles. He made a new brush at least every summer, or whenever the old one got soft and would not go through his hair.

A "puzzle" or toy was made from four long yucca leaves. They were placed so that they radiated out in four directions, their base ends overlapping. The puzzle was formed by folding each leaf, in turn, over the square formed by the overlapping ends and creasing the edges of the folds. The result was a kind of elastic chain. The tip ends were tied to secure the puzzle. Apache girls sometimes held contests to see who could make the longest chain, or to see who could make a puzzle in the shortest length of time. The finished puzzles were often given to small

children to beguile them into good humor. These yucca puzzles constituted one of the few playthings for babies and small children.

Sometimes yucca leaves were used like twine to mend sacks or other
items. The sharp point of the leaf tip functioned as a needle as the edges of
the tear were whipped together. Bundles of yucca leaves bound together at
the large ends were also used as brooms

FIREWOOD

Fuel for cooking and heating purposes was, of course, essential to a life
with any degree of comfort and was usually obtained from among a variety
of suitable woods available in most localities. It seems advisable here to
depart from the format of listing each wood used by genus in alphabetical
order. These woods have already been listed under other categories, and
it seems that a general discussion can best provide a picture of the Plains
Apache patterns in the selection and use of materials for firewood.

Contrary to popular belief, timber was relatively abundant on the
rolling plains of western Oklahoma, extending westward in narrow
strips along the numerous streams and watercourses. Furthermore, there
were stands of blackjack oak and post oak in many localities, and groves
of mesquite could be found beginning in the southwest portion of the
Apache country. Persimmon, western soapberry, and plum thickets containing many small to medium-sized trees grew on many hillsides and
well-watered draws, even on the open prairie. In the past, the Apache
typically pitched their camps in creek bottoms, where water and wood
were convenient for the routine activities of tribal life. Occasionally, as
when the tribe was on the move, camp might be made on the open prairie,
remote from trees and firewood. But even in these regions, some type of
plant material suitable for making fire was usually available. Louise
remembered hearing her mother say that when the Apache were camped
away from timber, they dug the roots of some kind of "weeds" to burn.
Louise thought her mother said they were sunflowers. But presumably the
dried up roots and woody stalks of a number of plants, as well as bison
chips, could be burned when regular firewood was not obtainable.

In the past, Apache women, assisted by their children, gathered
wood for their fires from among the resources in the area where they

Louise Saddleblanket making a child's "puzzle" with leaves of *Yucca glauca*, 1964.

were camped. They went out into the timber near camp and scavenged fallen wood or broke off dead limbs from trees, which they dragged back with rawhide ropes and piled near their tipis. More recently, Apache men, following the custom of rural whites, did most of the heavy work in providing firewood: chopping down trees and splitting and cutting the trunks and branches into suitable lengths.

At the time of our study most Plains Apache were still cooking their food and heating water over open wood fires when they came together to camp at their annual Blackfeet Dance celebration. The men went after firewood in pickup trucks, either scavenging dead wood from creek beds convenient to county roads or cutting wood from their land or the land of a relative. They dumped the wood in a pile by their families' camps and then the women chopped or broke it into suitable pieces for feeding the fire. Further, all the elders in our study had lived a good part of their lives in homes with wood-burning cook and heating stoves. Clearly, most adult Apache knew from personal experience the characteristics of the various woods available that make them suitable or not so desirable for use as firewood.

Which kind of wood was utilized seems to have been largely a function of what was available and convenient in any specific place, and almost any dry wood was burned when necessary. However, certain species were considered to be more desirable for cooking or heating than others. In general, good firewood for cooking meat and other foods was supposed to burn readily with a hot blaze and to form a good bed of long-lasting coals that gave out a lot of heat. Wood that burned away quickly, leaving only ashes, was practically useless for cooking meat. The Apache liked their fresh meat sliced fairly thin, one-fourth to one-half inch thick, and they liked to roast it over a bed of hot coals until it was well done. A blazing fire would char the outside of the meat, leaving the inside still rare.

Of the various woods available on the southern plains, the several oaks and the pecan, ash, western soapberry, and white elm seem to have been the favorites for firewood. Blackjack oak (*Quercus marilandica*) was especially prized for roasting meat because it burned readily, either green or dry, giving out a hot blaze and leaving a bed of long-lasting coals that radiated very intense heat. The elders maintained that black-jack oak imparted a better flavor to roast meat than any other wood. According to Fred, when green it was not difficult to chop and could be made up into firewood fairly easily. Dried out blackjack, however, was extremely difficult to handle, requiring, in Fred's words, "a good man and a good ax to make it up." Blackjack oak produced so much heat that it was not used by choice for the fires inside peyote tipis, as the participants would get uncomfortably warm. The other oaks also made good firewood. Post oak (*Q. stellata*), chinkapin oak (*Q. muehlenbergii*), Shumard's oak (*Q. shumardii*), and bur oak (*Q. macrocarpa*) all burned well and made plenty of coals. They were all used when convenient. Pecan

(*Carya illinoinensis*) also burned down to a good bed of coals. Louise said she liked pecan wood because it was easy to chop, but Rose thought it popped too much when it burned. Soapberry (*Sapindus saponaria*) made good firewood, putting out a lot of heat and leaving good coals. Concerning soapberry, Louise commented that if it was cut in the winter when the sap was down, it could be split easily for firewood or other purposes. Other trees were also easier to split in the winter than at other times.

Ash (*Fraxinus* sp.) made good firewood, too. It made good coals and, according to Fred, would burn green as well as when dry. Fred said ash was good to burn in peyote tipis when it was dry and after the bark was removed. The Apache term for ash, *ch'iłdíłgyǫǫts'ee*, means "wood splits easy," presumably referring to the relative ease with which its branches could be broken up. Dry redbud (*Cercis canadensis*) was also good to burn, as was dry dogwood (*Cornus drummondii*). Redbud was very brittle, and dead redbud trees could be pushed over easily when rotten, a fact no doubt well-known to Apache women scavenging the creek beds for firewood. Persimmon (*Diospyros virginiana*) was another wood that was easy to break up when dry, and it burned well, according to Rose. Hackberry (*Celtis laevigata*) and black locust (*Robinia pseudoacacia*) were also used for firewood. Rose said she did not like to burn hackberry because it popped, but Louise and Fred reported that dry hackberry made a good fire and was easy to chop up while green. Chittamwood (*Sideroxylon lanuginosum*) was also used occasionally. It burned somewhat like blackjack oak, making a hot fire and coals, according to Louise. Of the elms in the area, the white elm or American elm (*Ulmus americana*) was considered to make good firewood, but red elm (*Ulmus rubra*) was regarded as less satisfactory since it popped as it burned. Ray also stated that Chinese elm (*Ulmus pumila* L., Siberian elm), introduced into Oklahoma for shelterbelt plantings in 1912, burned well and did not pop. He said it was often used for firewood at peyote meetings.

Several native woods had characteristics making them undesirable for firewood, though any could be used if they were dry and better fuel was not available. Mulberry (*Morus rubra*) had a reputation for popping and scattering sparks. Cedar (*Juniperus virginiana*) was apparently never used as fuel for the same reason, and plum wood (*Prunus* sp.) was also supposed to pop badly. Cottonwood (*Populus deltoides*) and willow

(*Salix* sp.) were burned only if nothing else was available. Both of these soft woods burned quickly, leaving only ashes and no coals. However, Brant (1969: 122) noted that a pile of cottonwood bark was used to heat the rocks that were to be used in a sweat lodge ceremony. In fact, large chunks of dry bark from a number of trees could also be burned if necessary.

Fires were started with dry grass, leaves, or other easily flammable material, and larger twigs and sticks were added until the blaze was going well. In the past, some men started fires with rocks, presumably flints. Stems cut from dried bunches of big or little bluestem grasses used to be a favorite material for starting fires. In the days when bunches of bluestem were used as padding for beds, the women simply took a handful of their mattress to start up the breakfast fire. Ray said dried sunflower stalks were also used to start fires, and presumably other dried plant materials were also suitable for this purpose. In later times, of course, the Plains Apache used matches, paper, and occasionally an assist from a dousing with kerosene or white gasoline to get fires started in a hurry.

CHAPTER 6

Personal Care and Adornment

PLANTS USED IN PERSONAL CARE AND ADORNMENT

Artemisia

Artemisia filifolia Torr. Sand sagebrush, silvery wormwood.
Plains Apache: *tł'éłdisgóódedíchaahí*, "big sage."
The feathery branches of this plant, which is common in western Oklahoma, were sometimes used as a convenient substitute for toilet paper because they were soft. Other soft-leaved plants could also be used for this purpose.

Hierochloe

Hierochloe odorata (L.) P. Beauv. Sweetgrass.
Plains Apache: *tł'oshígołchįį*, "grass, it smells."
Sweetgrass, which was often used in ritual contexts as discussed in chapter 4, was also used as a sachet or perfume to store with clothes, imparting to them a pleasant, sweet fragrance. The long, pliable leaves and stems were plaited into braids of about one and one-half to two inches in diameter while still green, and tied at the ends. The braided grass was allowed to dry and then stored in a trunk or other container. It apparently retained its characteristic and well-liked odor indefinitely if kept dry. Both Rose and Connie May said they owned braids that they had had for many years and that still smelled as good as ever. For use, bits of grass were broken off the braid and placed in the folds of blankets

and clothing in storage. Sometimes the grass was moistened slightly first, or rubbed between the hands to release more of the odor. Sweetgrass was thought to be especially good for storing with buckskin clothes to keep them smelling fresh. Gertrude said her grandmother believed it kept moths and bugs out of her blankets, too.

Sweetgrass is not native to Oklahoma, but the Plains Apache obtained it by trade with other tribes or by purchase from commercial traders. A convenient substitute for sweetgrass was found in an introduced plant of European origin, white sweetclover (*Melilotus alba*, see next entry), the dried leaves and flowers of which were also used to perfume clothes.

Melilotus

Melilotus alba Medikus. White sweetclover.
Plains Apache: *tł'o'shígołchįį,* "grass, it smells."
The leaves and flowers of this plant were used in the same manner as sweetgrass to perfume and protect blankets, shawls, and other articles of clothing. A plant of European origin, it was accepted as a useful plant because its odor was similar to that of sweetgrass and it could be for the same personal purposes. It was not, however, used in a medicinal or ritual manner. The fresh leaves or stems of *Melilotus alba* were placed in the folds of garments or items stored in trunks. Clothes and blankets for dress occasions were treated with special care, being folded neatly and packed away with this or some other perfume so they would smell good when worn again. It was believed that these fragrant leaves would also repel moths and other insects. Sweetclover was apparently cut only while it was green, the amount needed for the year being gathered at that time. It could not be braided like sweetgrass. Sometimes bunches of sweet-clover plants were hung in tipis to freshen the air.

The odor of white sweetclover was not as strong and perhaps not as long-lasting as that of sweetgrass, which seemed to have been preferred for perfuming clothes. But the use of sweetclover increased as the plant became easier to obtain than sweetgrass. Connie May did not believe that her grandparents used white sweetclover as a perfume. She herself first learned of it from her husband, who had heard about it from some Comanche friends.

White sweetclover may have become naturalized on the southern plains by the late nineteenth century. Gilmore (1977: 39) reported that it was introduced onto the Omaha Reservation in 1856 by white missionaries, and the Omaha and Dakota soon began to use it as perfume. The Apache elders did not seem to be aware that it was not a native plant.

Monarda

Monarda fistulosa L. ssp. *fistulosa* var. *fistulosa*. Wild bergamot.
Plains Apache: *'it'ąąchoh*, "big leaf."
The lemon-scented leaves and flower heads of some members of this species constituted what the elders called, in English, "Indian perfume," which was used to impart an agreeable odor to the person and to clothes, blankets, and accessories. Indian perfume of good quality was one of the most treasured of personal possessions. It was highly regarded both for strictly aesthetic reasons and for its reputed power to attract members of the opposite sex as love partners.

Apparently the leaves of *Monarda fistulosa* varied widely in the character of their odor, and the Plains Apache were very particular in selecting leaves having the desired fragrance. Individual plants of *M. fistulosa* without this desired odor were regarded as "look-alikes" or "mates" to the "real perfume." They were called by at least four different terms: *'it'ąącho'be'ééside*, "it resembles perfume"; *zázayąąbít'ąącho'*, "coyote perfume"; *tł'o'dííchįįde*, "stinking grass"; and *chąąshįgółchįdee*, "it smells like feces." The latter term was never pronounced in the presence of relatives with whom one had a respect relationship, in which case one of the euphemisms was used instead. Connie May thought this term derived from the former use of the "fake" plants as substitutes for toilet paper, but Ray said it referred to the rank, disagreeable odor of the "fakes."

Other *Monarda* species, notably *M. citriodora* Cerv. and *M. punctata* L. var. *occidentalis* (Epl.) Palm. & Steyerm., were also called "mates" to Indian perfume, but the morphological distinctions were clear enough so that they were rarely, if ever, confused with the real plant. Botanically, these differ from *M. fistulosa* most noticeably in their prominent flower clusters, borne in stacks in axillary position, whereas the inflorescence of *M. fistulosa* is solitary and terminal. The really difficult problem lay in detecting the lemon-scented members within the *M. fistulosa* category. Here the morphological resemblance of "real" and "imitation" plants was so close that odor alone was the important distinguishing criterion. Persons had literally to "smell out" the real plant to distinguish it from the fake one. Obviously, a sharp sense of smell was a tremendous asset in this task, but the Apache believed that other attributes were also involved. Persons who had demonstrated their ability to collect good Indian perfume were respected and admired. They had little difficulty in disposing profitably of their surplus to those who could not locate their own perfume and thus had to buy it. Medicine men, who were supposedly more knowledgeable in herbal lore than most persons, were thought to have the greatest success in finding good perfume, but not all of them counted this ability as one of their accomplishments. Some medicine men, however, specialized in the preparation of love medicines, of which *M. fistulosa* was usually a key ingredient.

The real Indian perfume plant is rare in occurrence compared to its look-alikes. It grows in the shade of thickets and dry woods, either along creeks or in blackjack oak timber, often side by side with one of its close imitations. Persons often encountered it by accident when out in the country for other purposes. Louise said she once ran into it while riding a horse through some brush. Once found, a stand might be visited year after year, whenever more perfume was needed.

Concerning this plant, at least some Apache showed a unique concern over the future supply of the leaves and took some pains not to destroy a clump of the good-smelling Indian perfume by harvesting too much. The roots were never disturbed. Either some of the stems were broken off several inches above the ground, or the leaves alone were picked, leaving the stems behind. Louise said, "You break the leaves off; you don't break the stem. That way they'll be there every year." Individual practices regarding this attempt at conservation did vary, of course, but the idea seemed to be well established. There was also a fear that other persons would raid the source of supply, recklessly picking every stem, and for this reason the location of a stand of high-quality Indian perfume was often kept a closely guarded secret.

Indian perfume could be gathered any time there were leaves on the plant, or throughout most of the summer and early fall, though leaves from very young shoots were thought to have a weaker odor than older leaves. The inflorescence, a solitary terminal flower cluster, was also picked if present. Ray said extreme care must be used in gathering the leaves in order not to include any leaves or stems of the fake perfume. These had a strong and disagreeable odor, and a single leaf would detract from an otherwise perfect batch of real Indian perfume leaves. The leaves of the real perfume were dried and crumbled somewhat before being stored, and any stems were discarded. They were kept in a cloth or buckskin sack and packed away with other personal belongings.

The aromatic essence of the leaves was released most strongly when they were moistened. The usual method of using Indian perfume was to prepare an infusion of the dried leaves by soaking them in a small amount of water until it turned yellow. This liquid was then sprinkled on blankets and garments that were to be folded and stored away. This treatment would make them smell fresh and good when they were next used. A small amount of the infusion was also used on the person, especially the hair, being stroked on as the final touch in grooming for a dance or other special occasion. The dried leaves were also mixed at times with the aromatic seeds of another perfume plant called "birdseed," which, unfortunately, was not identified for this study. They were pounded up fine together and the infusion prepared from the mixed ingredients. Dried Indian perfume was sometimes simply chewed to softness, and the saliva spit out and applied to the hair and body. Dampened leaves could also be folded into clothing or packed with personal possessions. Garments for dress wear and ritual paraphernalia were especially apt to be treated with Indian perfume—dancing costumes, good shawls, peyote blankets, fans, feathers, and other items of a personal nature. Dried Indian perfume leaves were also carried on the person in a place where body heat and perspiration would accentuate their scent. Men often placed leaves in a shirt pocket; women usually carried theirs wrapped in a handkerchief tucked in the bosom of their dress.

The high esteem with which Indian perfume was regarded can hardly be overestimated. The elders were unanimous in their enthusiasm for its fragrance and long-lasting qualities, and they were proud to display samples from their personal horde. Interestingly enough, the elders were somewhat jealous of their own perfume and of their own ability to locate it

in the wild. They were prolific in their praises of specimens that they themselves had produced, but they were usually skeptical about specimens
collected by others. Often they would comment, as did Rose on one occasion, "That's just pretty near like it, but the real one smells better." Then
they would launch into a detailed description of the true plant. Rose also
expressed the consensus when she said, "It really smells good. You can
smell that perfume a long way off if you got that real kind." Louise added
an opinion from a former generation when she stated, "My grandma
wasn't around white people much. She don't like the way things changed
when the whites came. She said it was too hard a life. She always say in
those days they used Indian perfume all the time. When you'd pass a young
man he smell so nice. Nowadays you just smell like smoke, she say."

Perfume was indispensable to persons who were courting or in some
way trying to attract attention of potential lovers or sex partners. The
efficacy of Indian perfume in attracting persons of the opposite sex
seemed to be partly due to its reputation as an aphrodisiac and partly due
to the practice by persons seeking lovers of wearing it ostentatiously.
Really good, strong perfume was supposed to arouse sexual desire. Some
persons were specialists in preparing "love medicines." Persons who
were unable to obtain the favors of the man or woman they wanted could
go to a medicine man, if they could afford it, and obtain a love medicine
and instructions as to how to use it. Ray's father described the use of
these medicines thus: "Certain people had medicine to catch girls with.
They say they could make a girl crazy with it. Those people kept it quiet.
If you needed help to get a girl, you went to a medicine man who had
that power. You gave him something and he helped you. I think they
gave you a perfume to put on your clothes" (Bittle 1949). None of the
elders could provide any detailed information on the composition and
preparation of love medicines, but they agreed that the *M. fistulosa* and
perhaps "birdseed" were prime ingredients.

Apart from love medicines that were purchased from specialists,
Indian perfume alone could be used as a means of expressing romantic
interest or setting up an encounter. For this purpose the perfume had to
be worn at certain times and places, preferably when a potential couple
could speak together alone. A man interested in a certain woman would
arrange to come into her presence wearing good perfume and making

sure the breeze carried the scent in her direction. If she was interested in a liaison, she might comment on the fine perfume he was wearing, or ask him to make her a present of some. A more specific proposal would then follow. Ray said a woman might ask a man she wanted for some good perfume, using this request as a pretext for opening conversation and announcing her availability. If her interest were reciprocated, arrangements for a meeting could then be made.

Opuntia

Opuntia macrorhiza Engelm. Twistspine pricklypear.
Plains Apache: *góshchiish*, "red sticker."
The Plains Apache used long, stiff thorns of the pricklypear for piercing ears. Usually ear piercing took place in infancy, and though it could be done anytime, it was preferably done in the fall or in the spring. Ray's father said a good time was in the spring, when the plum bushes were in bloom, because then it did not hurt. But Louise, who was supposed to be good at this job, liked to do it in the fall. Formerly, both boys and girls had their ears pierced, but in recent years only baby girls underwent this operation.

The lobe of the ear was massaged first, to numb the area slightly, then the sharp-pointed thorn was thrust completely through in a single quick motion. The thorn was left in place, the ends being cut off close to the skin, until the wound healed. Tallow, or grease, was usually applied as a dressing. In a day or two, as the wound began to fester slightly, the thorn became loose and could be rotated without giving pain. It was turned in place often but not removed until the hole was completely healed. Grease was added periodically as a lubricant if necessary. When the ear lobes were healed, the thorns were removed and replaced with suitable earrings. Traditionally, the person who pierced the ears provided the first pair of earrings.

Sophora

Sophora secundiflora (Ortega) Lag. ex DC. Mescal bean.
Plains Apache: No term collected.

The mescal bean is a shrub or small tree that grows in the limestone regions of southwest Texas and eastern New Mexico. The fruit is a legume, or pod, containing very hard, bright red, glossy seeds. The Plains Apache obtained the seeds through travel or trade. The seeds were made into beads and used in a number of ways for personal adornment. A long strand of mescal beans, often combined with a similar strand of silver-colored beads, was worn as part of the costuming for the Blackfeet Dance and other tribal dances. Mescal beans might also decorate the ceremonial dress of tribal leaders and peyote ritual participants. Beads made of mescal beans were also used to decorate fringe on buckskin garments, and they were used in combination with other kinds of beads in necklaces, hair ties, fans, and other personal ornaments. Rose said, "They use some kind of berries—mescal berries. They look like peanuts. It doesn't grow around here, but in Texas around San Antonio and the border. They get ripe in October or September. They all over the ground in the spring. You pick out the good ones. Make holes in them and string them on buckskin. . . . The necklace goes around the neck and under one arm. A silver one [bandolier] goes with it."

Yucca

Yucca glauca Nutt. Soapweed yucca, "Indian cabbage."
Plains Apache: *dayígya*, "appears whitish."
The root of the yucca, which has saponaceous qualities, was used to shampoo the hair and, occasionally, to wash blankets or other articles of clothing. Thick, well-developed roots were best for this purpose. Since they were very long, digging them could be a considerable task, and for this reason they were often dug or pulled out from an embankment where the earth had washed away, leaving them partially exposed. They could be dug at any time but were considered to be at their best in mid-summer. Roots that were thick and produced the greatest amount of suds were said to be "fat." Connie May said that if left in the ground, the root dried up in the fall, though it could still be used if necessary.

Yucca roots were often stored for later use. The fresh root was peeled and the bark discarded. The remaining portion was then pounded flat and allowed to dry. Sometimes it was chopped into pieces several inches to one foot in length. The dried pieces of root were placed in a sack and hung up until needed.

For shampoo a handful of the root, either fresh or dried, was placed in a basin of water and agitated to make suds. This water was then used to wash the hair. The root particles could be left in the basin or scooped out after the suds had formed. Rose liked to strain all the roots out or else tie them in a cloth because she did not like bits and pieces of them to get in her hair. However, some people simply rinsed their hair after the sudsing until all of the particles were removed. The yucca shampoo left the hair clean and soft, and the older people thought it was better than white man's soap. Rose said it made the hair grow.

Connie May said yucca root was also used to wash clothes. The pounded root was placed in hot water, soaked, and agitated to make suds. Then the dirty clothes were added and scrubbed to make them come clean. She also said that her mother had even washed wool blankets satisfactorily with yucca root. Clothes and blankets washed with yucca were put through a rinse water to remove root particles clinging to them.

McAllister (1955: 158) noted that the body of a dead person was washed in yucca suds prior to burial.

OTHER PERFUMES

At least two and possibly more plants were also used as perfumes or ingredients in perfumes, but specimens and botanical identification of them could not be obtained in our study. One of these plants was known in English as "birdseed," although its Apache name, *bé'tsínílbaye*, meant "like something gray." This plant was reported to grow in a few localities in this part of Oklahoma, but it was mainly obtained through trade with the Wichita, Caddo, or Delaware. The significant part of the plant was the seed, abundant numbers of which were produced in large heads similar to those of broom corn in late summer. The seeds were small, black, and very fragrant when mixed with a little water. Birds were supposed to be very fond of them, hence the name "birdseed." The small seeds could be used alone or in combination with Indian perfume (*Monarda fistulosa*, see entry in this chapter). They were utilized in the same way as those of *M. fistulosa,* an infusion being prepared from the crushed seeds and sprinkled on clothes and personal accessories. This preparation was supposed to be especially good on feathers, and it was used often on peyote fans and other ritual items. It was not as long-lasting as Indian perfume, and the scent was said to be different, though very pleasant. "Birdseed" formed one ingredient of Connie May's stomach medicine (see entry on *Lithospermum* in chapter 4), and it may also have been used in the preparation of love medicines.

Another plant that the elders mentioned was "prairie dog perfume" (*dlo'zháyạbit'ạ́ạ́choo*), which may or may not have grown in the vicinity of prairie dog towns. The flowers of this plant were used as perfume and possibly also for medicine, but the elders' descriptions of it were vague and inconsistent and a specimen was not obtained. Louise said the use of this perfume was very old, and though she had heard of it, she had never encountered it. Grinnell (1962:189–90) mentioned a prairie dog perfume used by the Cheyenne, but any possible connection with that of the Plains Apache has yet to be established.

Conclusion

In the preceding chapters I have presented data on the traditional plant knowledge of the Plains Apache, a typical hunting and gathering tribe with several hundred years of experience living on the Great Plains. The data presented were those that were recoverable from six tribal elders in the mid 1960s and illustrate Plains Apache plant usage for approximately the period 1890 to 1950, with some usages undoubtedly being much older. I have listed and described the culturally significant plants and the cultural contexts in which the plants were used. I have also presented information on Plains Apache beliefs, concepts, and attitudes about the plant world.

I do not claim that the materials here are a complete listing of plants known and used by the Plains Apache. My principal fieldwork was limited to eight weeks each in the summers of 1963 and 1964. Certain areas of possible inquiry were not addressed, such as which plants might have been important as fodder for bison and livestock. However, the data are complete enough to show that the Plains Apache, and no doubt other bison-hunting Plains tribes, utilized plants to an extent rarely appreciated by early ethnographers.

During our field work, specimens of over 190 plants were collected from within parts of Caddo, Kiowa, and Comanche counties in southwestern Oklahoma. More than one hundred of the collected plants were recognized by the elders as having some significance in the traditional culture. In addition to the useful plants identified from the fieldwork specimens, the total inventory of Plains Apache useful plants presented here includes a number of plants identified in other ways.

TABLE 1. Summary of Plants and Fungi Used by the Plains Apache

Total number of species: plants (110) and fungi (2)	112
Total number of species native to North America	108
Total number of species native to Oklahoma	102
Species used as edible plants	47
Species used as ritual and medicinal plants	40
Species used for material culture	43
Species used for fuel	11
Species used for personal care and adornment	8
Species with multiple uses	26
Total number of genera	87
Total number of families	49

Only plants and fungi with verifiable Plains Apache uses are included in this table. Plants classified as "mates" or "weeds" are not included.

The botanical nomenclature for peyote (*Lophophora williamsii*), mescal bean (*Sophora secundiflora*), sweetgrass (*Hierochloe odorata*), pinyon pine (*Pinus edulis*), and chokecherry (*Prunus virginiana*) is well known. All of these plants were used by the Plains Apache. Some additional plants were identified on the basis of descriptions by elders in combination with plant profile and distribution data. These include groundnut (*Apios americana*), groundplum milkvetch (*Astragalus crassicarpus*), sneezeweed (*Helenium microcephalum*), graybark grape (*Vitis cinerea*), sand grape (*Vitis rupestris*), and golden currant (*Ribes aureum*). Specimens of White Sands sage (*Poliomintha incana*) and Porter's licoriceroot (*Ligusticum porterii*) were obtained and identified after the initial fieldwork as described in the entries for these plants in the text.

Several other culturally significant plants were described by the elders, but specimens could not be found and the descriptions were not sufficient for even tentative botanical identification. These included two food plants, a root called "Indian sweet potato" (*sáayód*) and another root called "Indian turnip" (*nádests'aaγe*). The latter was different from the "Indian turnip" identified as *Pediomelum esculentum* (*tł'otł'ą́ą́*). Other unidentified plants were those used as components in "sneezing medicine" and "birdseed perfume." There exists some possibility that these plants could yet be identified through further study.

Table 2. List of Plants and Fungi Used by the Plains Apache

Division, Genus, Species	Family	Common Name	Ethnobotanical Category	Plant Part Used
Fungi				
Lycoperdon spp.	Lycoperdaceae	Puffball	Ritual/medicinal	Spore mass
Unknown	Unknown	"Bracket fungi"	Ritual/medicinal	Fruiting body
Horsetails				
Equisetum hyemale L.	Equisetaceae	Scouringrush horsetail	Material culture	Stem
Flowering Plants				
Aesculus glabra Willd. var. *arguta* (Buckley) B. L. Rob.	Hippocastanaceae	Ohio buckeye	Material culture	Seed
Allium canadense L. var. *fraseri* Ownbey	Lilliaceae	Fraser meadow garlic	Edible	Bulb, leaf
Allium drummondii Regel	Lilliaceae	Drummond's onion	Edible	Bulb, leaf
Allium perdulce S. V. Fraser	Lilliaceae	Plains onion	Edible	Bulb, leaf
Ambrosia psilostachya DC.	Asteraceae	Cuman ragweed	Ritual/medicinal	Leaf
Ambrosia trifida L. var. *texana* Scheele	Asteraceae	Texan great ragweed	Material culture	Whole plant
Amphiachyris dracunculoides (DC.) Nutt. (= *Gutierrezia dracunculoides* (DC.) S. F. Blake	Asteraceae	Prairie broomweed	Ritual/medicinal	Stem, leaf
Andropogon gerardii Vitman	Poaceae	Big bluestem	Material culture	Stem (culm), leaf
			Ritual/medicinal	Stem (culm), leaf
Apios americana Medik (= *Glycine apios* L.).	Fabaceae	Groundnut	Edible	Tuber
Artemisia filifolia Torr.	Asteraceae	Sand sagebrush	Material culture	Stem, leaf
			Personal	Stem, leaf
Artemisia ludoviciana Nutt. ssp. *mexicana* (Willd. ex Spreng.) D. D. Keck	Asteraceae	White sagebrush	Ritual/medicinal	Stem, leaf
Asclepias sp.	Asclepiadaceae	Milkweed	Edible	Immature fruit

Table 2. List of Plants and Fungi Used by the Plains Apache (*continued*)

Division, Genus, Species	Family	Common Name	Ethnobotanical Category	Plant Part Used
Asclepias stenophylla A. Gray	Asclepiadaceae	Slimleaf milkweed	Ritual/medicinal	Root
Asclepias tuberosa L.	Asclepiadaceae	Butterfly milkweed	Ritual/medicinal	Root
Astragalus crassicarpus Nutt.	Fabaceae	Groundplum milkvetch	Ritual/medicinal	Root
Baptisia bracteata Muhl. ex Elliot. var. *leucophaea* (Nutt.) Kartesz & Gandhi	Fabaceae	Longbract wild indigo	Material culture	Fruit (legume)
Bouteloua curtipendula (Michx.) Torr.	Poaceae	Sideoats grama	Ritual/medicinal	Leaf
Callirhoe involucrata (Torr. & A. Gray) A. Gray	Malvaceae	Purple poppymallow	Edible	Root
Carya illinoinensis (Wangenh.) K. Koch	Juglandaceae	Pecan	Edible	Seed
			Material Culture	Wood
			Fuel	Wood
Celtis laevigata Willd.	Ulmaceae	Sugarberry	Edible	Fruit
			Material culture	Wood
			Fuel	Wood
Cocculus carolinus (L.) DC.	Menispermaceae	Carolina coralbead	Edible	Fruit
Cornus drummondii C. A. Mey.	Cornaceae	Roughleaf dogwood	Material culture	Wood
Crataegus sp.	Rosaceae	Hawthorn	Edible	Fruit
Cucurbita foetidissima Kunth	Cucurbitaceae	Missouri gourd	Ritual/medicinal	Root, stem, leaf, fruit
Cuscuta sp.	Cuscutaceae	Dodder	Ritual/medicinal	Whole plant
Cyperus setigerus Torr. & Hook.	Cyperaceae	Lean flatsedge	Edible	Stem (culm) base
Dalea enneandra Nutt.	Fabaceae	Nineanther prairie clover	Ritual/medicinal	Stem
Diospyros virginiana L.	Ebenaceae	Common persimmon	Edible	Fruit
Echinacea angustifolia DC.	Asteraceae	Blacksamson echinacea	Ritual/medicinal	Root
Eriogonum longifolium Nutt.	Polygonaceae	Longleaf buckwheat	Ritual/medicinal	Root
Escobaria missouriensis (Sweet) D.R. Hunt (= *Coryphantha missouriensis* (Sweet) Britton & Rose) and (= *Mammillaria missouriensis* Sweet)	Cactaceae	Missouri foxtail cactus	Edible	Fruit

Table 2. List of Plants and Fungi Used by the Plains Apache (*continued*)

Division, Genus, Species	Family	Common Name	Ethnobotanical Category	Plant Part Used
Fraxinus sp.	Oleaceae	Ash	Material culture	Wood
			Fuel	Wood
Gaura coccinea Nutt. ex Pursh	Onagraceae	Scarlet beeblossom	Material culture	Stem
Gymnocladus dioicus (L.) K. Koch	Fabaceae	Kentucky coffeetree	Material culture	Wood, seed
Helenium microcephalum DC.	Asteraceae	Smallhead sneezeweed	Ritual/medicinal	Inflorescence
Helianthus sp.	Asteraceae	Sunflower	Material culture	Whole plant
Hierochloe odorata (L.) P. Beauv.*	Poaceae	Sweetgrass	Ritual/medicinal	Stem (culm), leaf
			Personal	
Ipomoea leptophylla Torr.	Convolvulaceae	Bush morning-glory	Ritual/medicinal	Root
Juglans microcarpa Berl. var. *microcarpa* (= *Juglans repestris* Engelm.)	Juglandaceae	Little walnut	Edible	Seed
			Material culture	Wood
			Personal	Seed
Juglans nigra L.	Juglandaceae	Black walnut	Edible	Seed
			Material culture	Wood
Juniperus pinchotii Sudw.	Cupressaceae	Pinchot's juniper	Ritual/medicinal	Leaf
Juniperus virginiana L.	Cupressaceae	Eastern redcedar	Material culture	Wood
Lespedeza capitata Michx.	Fabaceae	Roundhead lespedeza	Edible	Leaf
			Ritual/medicinal	Leaf
Liatris punctata Hook.	Asteraceae	Dotted blazing star	Edible	Root
			Ritual/medicinal	Root
Ligusticum porteri J. M. Coult. & Rose var. *porteri**	Apiaceae	Porter's licoriceroot	Ritual/medicinal	Root
Lithospermum incisum Lehm.	Boraginaceae	Narrowleaf stoneseed	Ritual/medicinal	Root
Lophophora williamsii (Lem. ex Salm-Dyck) J. M.Coult.*	Cactaceae	Peyote	Ritual/medicinal	Whole plant
Lygodesmia juncea (Pursh) D. Don ex Hook.	Asteraceae	Rush skeletonplant	Ritual/medicinal	Stem
Maclura pomifera (Raf.) C. K. Schneid.	Moraceae	Osage orange, bois d'arc	Material culture	Wood

Table 2. List of Plants and Fungi Used by the Plains Apache (*continued*)

Division, Genus, Species	Family	Common Name	Ethnobotanical Category	Plant Part Used
Matelea biflora (Raf.) Woodson	Asclepiadaceae	Star milkvine	Edible	Immature fruit
			Ritual/medicinal	Root
Melilotus alba Medikus †	Fabaceae	White sweetclover	Personal	Stem, leaf, flower
Mentzelia nuda (Pursh) Torr. & A. Gray var. *stricta* (Osterh.) Harrington	Loasaceae	Bractless blazing star	Material culture	Leaf
Mimosa microphylla Dryand. (=*Schrankia uncinata* Willd.)	Fabaceae	Littleleaf sensitive-briar	Ritual/medicinal	Flower
Monarda fistulosa L. ssp. *fistulosa* var. *fistulosa*	Lamiaceae	Wild bergamot	Personal	Leaf, flower
Morus rubra L.	Moraceae	Red mulberry	Edible	Fruit
			Material culture	Wood
			Ritual/medicinal	Root
			Fuel	Fuel
Nasturtium officinale W. T. Aiton †	Brassicaceae	Watercress	Edible	Leaf
Nelumbo lutea Willd.	Nelumbonaceae	American lotus	Edible	Rhizome, seed
Opuntia macrorhiza Engelm	Cactaceae	Twistspine pricklypear	Edible	Fruit
			Ritual/medicinal	Stem (pads)
			Personal	Spine
Paronychia virginica Spreng.	Caryophyllaceae	Yellow nailwort	Material culture	Leaf
			Ritual/medicinal	Whole plant
Pediomelum esculentum (Pursh) Rydb. (= *Psoralea esculenta* Pursh)	Fabaceae	Large Indian breadroot	Edible	Root
Phytolacca americana L.	Phytolaccaceae	American pokeweed	Edible	Stem, leaf
			Material culture	Fruit
Pinus edulis Engelm.	Pinaceae	Twoneedle pinyon	Edible	Seed, resin
Pinus sp.*	Pinaceae	Pine	Material culture	Wood
Plantago patagonica Jacq. (= *Plantago pursii* Roem. and Schult.)	Plantaginaceae	Wooly plantain	Material culture	Inflorescence

Table 2. List of Plants and Fungi Used by the Plains Apache (*continued*)

Division, Genus, Species	Family	Common Name	Ethnobotanical Category	Plant Part Used
Plantago wrightiana Decne.	Plantaginaceae	Wright's plantain	Material culture	Inflorescence
Poliomintha incana (Torr.) A. Gray *	Lamiaceae	Frosted mint	Ritual/medicinal	Stem, leaf, flower
Populus deltoides Bartram ex Marsh.	Salicaceae	Eastern cottonwood	Material culture	Wood
Proboscidea louisianica (Mill.) Thell.	Martyniaceae	Ram's horn	Edible	Seed
			Ritual/medicinal	Seed
Prosopis glandulosa Torr. *var. glandulosa*	Fabaceae	Honey mesquite	Edible	Fruit (legume), seed
Prunus angustifolia Marsh.	Rosaceae	Chickasaw plum	Edible	Fruit
Prunus gracilis Engelm. & A. Gray	Rosaceae	Oklahoma plum	Edible	Fruit
Prunus mexicana S. Watson	Rosaceae	Mexican plum	Edible	Fruit
Prunus virginiana L.	Rosaceae	Chokecherry	Edible	Fruit
Psoralidium tenuiflorum (Pursh) Rydb. (= *Psoralea tenuiflora* Pursh)	Fabaceae	Slimflower scurfpea	Material culture	Stem
Pyrrhopappus grandiflorus (Nutt.) Nutt.	Asteraceae	Tuberous desert-chicory	Edible	Tuber
Quercus macrocarpa Michx.	Fagaceae	Bur oak	Material culture	Wood
			Fuel	Wood
Quercus marilandica Münchh.	Fagaceae	Blackjack oak	Ritual/medicinal	Leaf
			Fuel	Wood
Quercus muehlenbergii Engelm.	Fagaceae	Chinkapin oak	Ritual/medicinal	Leaf
			Fuel	Wood
Quercus shumardii Buckley	Fagaceae	Shumard's oak	Material culture	Wood
			Fuel	Wood
Quercus spp.	Fagaceae	Oak	Edible	Nut (acorn)
Quercus stellata Wangenh.	Fagaceae	Post oak	Material culture	Wood
			Fuel	Wood
Quincula lobata (Torr.) Raf. (= *Physalis lobata* Torr.)	Solanaceae	Chinese lantern	Material culture	Fruit

Table 2. List of Plants and Fungi Used by the Plains Apache (*continued*)

Division, Genus, Species	Common Name	Family	Ethnobotanical Category	Plant Part Used
Rhus aromatica Aiton	Fragrant sumac	Anacardiaceae	Edible	Fruit
Rhus glabra L.	Smooth sumac	Anacardiaceae	Ritual/medicinal	Leaf
Ribes aureum Pursh var. *villosum* DC.	Golden currant	Grossulariaceae	Edible	Fruit
Robinia pseudoacacia L.	Black locust	Fabaceae	Material culture	Wood
Rubus spp.	Blackberry	Rosaceae	Edible	Fruit
Salix interior Rowlee	Sandbar willow	Salicaceae	Material culture	Stem, bark, leaf
Salix nigra Marsh.	Black willow	Salicaceae	Material culture	Stem, bark, leaf
Sapindus saponaria L. var. *drummondii* (Hook. & Arn.) L. D. Benson	Western soapberry	Sapindaceae	Material culture / Ritual/medicinal	Wood / Bark
Schizachyrium scoparium (Michx.) Nash var. *scoparium* (= *Andropogon scoparius* Michx.)	Little bluestem	Poaceae	Material culture / Ritual/medicinal	Stem (culm), leaf / Stem (culm), leaf
Sideroxylon lanuginosum Michx. (= *Bumelia lanuginosa* (Michx.) Pers.)	Gum bully, chittamwood	Sapotaceae	Edible / Fuel	Sap, fruit / Wood
Silphium laciniatum L.	Compassplant	Asteraceae	Edible	Sap
Solanum dimidiatum Raf.	Western horsenettle	Solanaceae	Material culture	Fruit
Solidago sp.	Goldenrod	Asteraceae	Ritual/medicinal	Leaf
Sophora secundiflora (Ortega) Lag. ex DC.*	Mescal bean	Fabaceae	Material culture / Personal	Seed / Seed
Sorghum halepense (L.) Pers. †	Johnsongrass	Poaceae	Material culture	Stem (culm), leaf
Teucrium canadense L.	Canada germander	Lamiaceae	Ritual/medicinal	Leaf
Thelesperma filifolium (Hook.) A. Gray var. *intermedium* (Rydb.) Shinners	Stiff greenthread	Asteraceae	Edible	Seed
Typha sp.	Cattail	Typhaceae	Edible / Ritual/medicinal	Rhizome / Pollen
Ulmus americana L.	American elm	Ulmaceae	Material culture / Fuel	Wood / Wood

Table 2. List of Plants and Fungi Used by the Plains Apache (*continued*)

Division, Genus, Species	Family	Common Name	Ethnobotanical Category	Plant Part Used
Ulmus pumila L. †	Ulmaceae	Siberian elm	Fuel	Wood
Ulmus rubra Muhl.	Ulmaceae	Slippery elm	Edible	Inner bark, sap
			Material culture	Wood
Vernonia baldwinii Torr.	Asteraceae	Baldwin's ironweed	Material culture	Stem, leaf
Viburnum rufidulum Raf.	Caprifoliaceae	Rusty blackhaw	Edible	Fruit
Vitis cinerea (Engelm.) Engelm. ex Millard	Vitaceae	Graybark grape	Edible	Fruit
Vitis riparia Michx.	Vitaceae	Riverbank grape	Edible	Fruit
Vitis rupestris Scheele	Vitaceae	Sand grape	Edible	Fruit
Vitis spp.	Vitaceae	Grape	Material culture	Stem, wood
Vitis vulpina L.	Vitaceae	Frost grape	Edible	Fruit
Yucca glauca Nutt.	Agavaceae	Soapweed yucca	Material culture	Flower, immature
			Personal	inflorescence, leaf

Note: All species are native to Oklahoma unless otherwise indicated.

* Not native to Oklahoma

† Not native to North America

The Plains Apache elders, in describing the uses of plants, were also able to provide a wealth of detail pertaining to many aspects of the traditional culture, including food preparation and consumption, material culture, concepts of health and illness, doctoring and medicines, religious and ceremonial activity, and personal care and adornment. Their information came from personal experience as well as from listening to their own elders talk about life in the reservation or pre-reservation periods.

Finally, the data collected allowed some generalizations to be made concerning underlying concepts and beliefs about the plant world. The Plains Apache regarded plants as parts of the larger world of nature, which encompassed all natural phenomena. In their language, they had no single term equivalent to the English word "plant," although they did have terms for a few broad categories of plants. These were *tł'oh*, "grass"; *xosh*, "thorny plant"; *jee*, "food" or "fruit"; *ch'ił*, "brush"; *-ko̩'é* and *–ch'ish*, "wood" or "tree"; *tł'oł*, "vine"; and *datį̨́įzhił*, "tall, nonwoody plants." The Apache felt themselves to be an integral part of nature, for which they had a deep respect and reverence. There was an inherent harmony and balance in the natural order. Different aspects of nature, including plants, existed for the well-being of humankind. All plants were potentially useful, and the Apache respected persons who, through experience or personal quest, learned how to find and use plants for the benefit of the people. They did not consciously try to change nature. They strove to adapt to it, to maintain harmony with it, and to commune with its various aspects through prayer and ritual.

The Plains Apache also believed that plants existed in pairs. Every "real" plant had one or more "mates" or "look-alikes." For example, the "real" Indian perfume (*Monarda fistulosa*) had a mate called "coyote perfume" (*Monarda punctata* and *Monarda citriodora*). The mate for the "real" Indian turnip (*Pediomelum esculentum*) was a related species, *Pediomelum cuspidatum*, and the mate for Indian tea (*Lespedeza capitata*) was *Lespedeza stuevei*. Again, the Apache respected persons who could unerringly distinguish the "real" plant, the useful plant, from its "look-alikes."

The fact that the elders could recall and supply detailed information on 112 plants that were of significance in the traditional culture, plus names and information on certain other plants, suggests that the Plains

Apache had a very rich ethnobotanical heritage deriving from many generations of residence on the Great Plains. The earliest European explorers of the Plains, the Spanish, made little mention of plants used by the peoples they encountered, being preoccupied with conquest and the quest for gold. Yet, Juan de Oñate, visiting the Canadian River in the summer of 1601, wrote: "Here we were met by some Indians of the nation called Apache, who welcomed us with demonstrations of peace. . . . They brought us along some small fruit, black and yellow, which abounds everywhere along the river. These were the size of small tomatoes and gave every indication of being healthful, for although we ate them without restraint no one suffered any ill effects" (Schroeder 1974: 235).

When Oñate ventured even further east on the plains, he met another nomadic group. They "were moving their camp to follow the cattle, whose meat they eat without bread, but with roots and fruits" (Schroeder 1974: 237). Thus, even the preoccupied Spaniards could not help but notice that wild plant foods were of importance in the diet of nomadic, bison-hunting groups.

No doubt many other plant species were formerly known and used, especially in pre-reservation times when the Plains Apache resided in or traveled to other regions of the Great Plains. Other regions would have different conditions of climate, elevation, and topography, with plant assemblages differing in composition from those of southwestern Oklahoma. However, the genius of the Plains Apache was their ability to survive in new environments and under changing pressures. Albert H. Schroeder (1974: 40), speaking of the Apacheans in general, commented, "The entire history of the Apaches is concerned with population shifts and adaptation to new situations." In a different geographical setting, the Plains Apache no doubt knew and used plant species other than those described here. In a region new to them, they would find, or learn of, plants with the qualities they needed and fit them into their own cultural framework.

Comprehensive comparison of the ethnobotanical data obtained from the Plains Apache with similar data from other Plains tribes was beyond the scope of this study, although I have presented some information on the use of certain plants by other tribes. I believe that the data here should be of value for a variety of future comparative studies.

Several ethnobotanical resources for other southern plains tribes already exist. Vestal and Schultes (1939), in their study of "The Economic Botany of the Kiowa Indians," listed 105 plants of significance to the Kiowa. Their list included some plants, mainly grasses, that were valued exclusively as fodder for horses. Their list also included the cultigens maize and bottle gourds, as well as a few plants used only as decorations. Their data were collected in the 1930s from two aged women and a seventy-year-old medicine man and peyote leader. Carlson and Jones (1940) discussed the uses of plants by the Comanche Indians in their paper, "Some Notes on Uses of Plants by the Comanche Indians." They listed forty-seven identified useful plants and fifteen unidentified useful plants. Their data were collected in 1933 from non–English speaking elders with the help of an interpreter. George Bird Grinnell, whose close association with the Cheyenne began in 1890 and lasted for many years, devoted a full chapter to useful plants in his excellent two-volume monograph, *The Cheyenne Indians*, first published in 1923. He listed ninety-four plants used as food, medicine, and material culture items, along with the Cheyenne names for the plants and much detail on plant use. Many other ethnobotanical resources now exist, including many items on the Internet.

The history of the Plains Apache reveals a people with remarkable survival and adaptive skills. A small tribe residing on the Great Plains since at least the mid-sixteenth century, they knew well how to exploit both the plant and the animal resources available to them. However, most ethnographers of Plains tribes have stressed the importance of the bison, giving only limited attention to the use of plants. This study shows that the Plains Apache and, by extension, other Plains tribes made extensive use of a wide variety of plants for food, medicines, items of material culture, firewood, ritual accompaniments, and personal care.

Although this ethnobotany could probably be expanded in some respects, most of the work here would be impossible to replicate. The elders who were the custodians of the language and traditional culture are gone. The last person who could speak the language with any fluency, a man ninety-seven years old, died in February of 2008. Thus, the first-hand sources of Plains Apache plant terminology no longer exist. A number of traditionally minded Apache do care deeply about their history and former way of life. Insofar as is possible in the modern world, they make an effort to keep certain traditions alive. Possibly several families own and care for some artifacts from the past, including, perhaps, some small cloth or buckskin sacks containing powdered herbs that no one knows how to use, or feels that they have a right to use.

The Apache still show a preference for traditional American Indian foods, such as maize and pumpkin and including also wild plums, grapes, chokecherries, and pinyon nuts. The fruits are now mainly eaten fresh or in the form of jellies and jams rather than in dried form. Skunkberries (*Rhus aromatica*) and Indian tea (*Lespedeza capitata*) may occasionally be served to young people, mainly to show them something of what their grandparents ate. The edible roots of wild plants such as Indian turnip (*Pediomelum esculentum*) are dug rarely, if at all, because they are now exceedingly difficult to locate and time-consuming to process. The modern Apache, like other Americans, are a busy people and have little time for labor-intensive food preparation.

The Plains Apache share with other tribes in a Pan-Indian culture in which regional styles of dance, dress, and behavior have emerged from particular tribal styles. The Apache travel widely to attend the dances and ceremonials of other tribes. Yet, within this Pan-Indian milieu they still maintain a distinct social and cultural identity. They have their own tribal complex, elected officials, social activities, and programs of education, health care, and economic development. Plains Apache culture has changed and evolved over the decades, but it has not disappeared. To outsiders the most visible aspect of the surviving traditional culture is the Manatidie, or Blackfeet Dance, with its ceremonial fur-wrapped staffs, distinctive songs, and colorful costuming. The men dancers wear bandoliers of mescal bean beads, have small pouches of aromatic herbs such as sage or Indian perfume secured to their costume regalia, and carry feather fans bearing the aroma of mountain cedar leaves, Indian perfume, or sweetgrass. At the annual Blackfeet Dance gatherings, willow arbors may still be seen among the now more common canvas or plastic canopies used for shade. One or more tipis, erected on frames of cedar poles and secured with pegs of western soapberry wood, may be prominent at the entrances to the dance grounds.

Peyote meetings also continue to be an important form of religious expression. The scents of sage and mountain cedar incense pervade the interior of the tipi, mixing with the scents of tobacco and wood smoke. Drummers use drumsticks carved of the heartwood of black walnut, and the ritual participants keep their peyote paraphernalia in rectangular boxes often constructed of cedar wood.

The Plains Apache elders who participated in this study have left an enduring legacy for their descendants and for all persons interested in American Indian life and culture. They have helped preserve an important part of their traditional knowledge, identifying many significant plants and explaining in detail the cultural contexts surrounding their use. They have also offered their belief as to how the plant world should be approached: Nature is all-encompassing, powerful, and awesome, and it should be treated with thoughtful, even prayerful, respect. When respect is lost, when resources are squandered, things can go wrong. The Plains Apache believe they are an integral part of nature and should coexist in harmony with plants, animals, and other natural phenomena. While the Apache elders may not have envisioned the world of the twenty-first century in which their descendants live, their message is worthy of consideration. They may properly be thanked for their willingness to share their knowledge and wisdom. *Ahó! Ahó!*

References

Abel, Annie Heloise. 1939. *Tabeau's narrative of Loisel's expedition to the upper Missouri.* Norman: University of Oklahoma Press.

Bailey, R. G., P. E. Avers, T. King, and W. H. McNab, eds. 1994. *Ecoregions and subregions of the United States* [map]. Washington, D.C.: U.S. Department of Agriculture Forest Service.

Bittle, William E. 1949–1964. Unpublished Kiowa-Apache field notes.

———. 1954. The peyote ritual: Kiowa-Apache. *Papers in Anthropology* (University of Oklahoma) 2:69–78.

———. 1956. The position of Kiowa-Apache in the Apachean group. Ph.D. diss., Department of Anthropology, University of California, Berkeley.

———. 1960. Curative aspects of peyotism. *Bios* 31:140–48.

———. 1962. The *Manatidie*: A focus for Kiowa Apache tribal identity. *Plains Anthropologist* 7:152–163.

———. 1963. Kiowa-Apache. In *Studies in the Athapascan languages,* by Harry Hoijer and others. University of California Publications in Linguistics, vol. 29. Berkeley and Los Angeles: University of California Press.

———. 1971. A brief history of the Kiowa Apache. *Papers in Anthropology* (University of Oklahoma) 12 (1): 1–34.

Bittle, William E., and Julia A. Jordan. 1963–1964. Unpublished field notes.

Blankinship, J.W. 1905. *Native economic plants of Montana.* Bozeman: Montana Agricultural College Experiment Station, bulletin no. 56.

Brant, Charles S. 1950. Peyotism among the Kiowa-Apache and neighboring tribes. *Southwestern Journal of Anthropology* 6 (2): 212–22.

Brant, Charles S., ed. 1969. *Jim Whitewolf: The life of a Kiowa Apache Indian.* New York: Dover Publications.

Bross, Michael Grantham. 1962. The Kiowa-Apache body concept in relation to health. Master's thesis, Department of Anthropology, University of Oklahoma.

Bruner, W. E. 1931. The vegetation of Oklahoma. *Ecological Monographs* 1:99–188.

Carlson, Gustav G., and Volney H. Jones. 1940. Some notes on uses of plants by the Comanche Indians. *Papers of the Michigan Academy of Science, Arts and Letters* 24:517–42.

Curtis, N. M., W. E. Hams, K. S. Johnson, C. C. Branson, S. E. Marcher, and J. F. Roberts. 1972. *Geology and earth resources of Oklahoma*. Oklahoma City: Oklahoma Game and Fish Department.

DeMallie, Raymond, ed. 2001. *Plains*. Vol. 13 of *Handbook of North American Indians*, ed. by W. Sturtevant. Washington, D.C.: Smithsonian Institution Press.

Elmore, Francis H. 1944. *Ethnobotany of the Navajo*. University of New Mexico and School of American Research Monograph No. 8. Santa Fe.

Ford, Richard I. 1978. Ethnobotany: Historical diversity and synthesis. In *The Nature and Status of Ethnobotany*, edited by R. I. Ford, 33–49. Museum of Anthropology Anthropological Paper no. 67. Ann Arbor: University of Michigan.

Foster, Morris W., and Martha McCollough. 2001. Plains Apache. In *Handbook of North American Indians*. Vol. 13, pt. 2, *Plains,* edited by Raymond J. DeMallie, 926–940. Washington, D.C.: Smithsonian Institution Press.

Gilmore, Melvin Randolph. [1919] 1977. *Uses of plants by the Indians of the Missouri River region*. Lincoln: University of Nebraska Press.

Goodman, George J. 1958. *Spring flora of central Oklahoma*. Norman: University of Oklahoma Duplicating Service.

Great Plains Flora Association. 1986. *Flora of the Great Plains*. Lawrence: University Press of Kansas.

Grinnell, George Bird. 1961 [1889]. *Pawnee hero stories and folk-tales*. Lincoln: University of Nebraska Press.

———. 1962 [1923]. *The Cheyenne Indians: Their history and ways of life*. New Haven, Conn.: Yale University Press.

Gunnerson, Dolores A. 1956. The Southern Athabascans: Their arrival in the Southwest. *El Palacio* 63 (11-12): 346–65.

———. 1974. *The Jicarilla Apaches: A study in survival*. DeKalb, Ill.: Northern Illinois University Press.

Gunnerson, James H., and Dolores A. Gunnerson. 1971. Apachean culture: A study in unity and diversity. In *Apachean Culture History and Ethnology*, edited by Keith H. Basso and Morris E. Opler, 7–27. Anthropological Papers of the University of Arizona, 21. Tucson: University of Arizona Press.

Haines, Francis. 1938a. Where did the Plains Indians get their horses? *American Anthropologist* 40 (3): 112–17.

———. 1938b. The northward spread of horses among the Plains Indians. *American Anthropologist* 40 (3): 429–37.

Hoagland, B. W. 2000. The vegetation of Oklahoma: A classification for landscape mapping and conservation planning. *The Southwestern Naturalist* 45:385–420.

Hoagland, B. W., A. K. Buthod, I. H. Butler, P. H. C. Crawford, A. H. Udasi, W. J. Elisens, and R. J. Tyrl. 2004. Oklahoma vascular plants database. www.coordinatesolutions.com/ovpd/ovpd.aspx. Oklahoma Biological Survey, University of Oklahoma, Norman.

Hoijer, Harry. 1938. The Southern Athapascan languages. *American Anthropologist* 40 (1): 75–87.

———. 1971. The position of the Apachean languages in the Athapaskan stock. In *Apachean Culture, History and Ethnology*, edited by Keith H. Basso and Morris E. Opler, 3–6. Anthropological Papers of the University of Arizona, vol. 21. Tucson: University of Arizona Press.

Jablow, Joseph. 1950. *The Cheyenne in Plains Indian trade relations, 1795–1840.* Monographs of the American Ethnological Society, vol. 19. Seattle: University of Washington Press.

Jones, David Earle. 1968. Comanche plant medicine. *Papers in Anthropology* (University of Oklahoma) 9:1–12.

———. 1984 [1972]. *Sanapia: Comanche medicine woman.* Long Grove, Ill.: Waveland Press.

Jordan, Julia A. 1965. Ethnobotany of the Kiowa-Apache. Master's thesis, Department of Anthropology, University of Oklahoma.

———. 1964–1972. Unpublished field notes.

Jordan, Julia A., with Wayne Elisens and Richard Thomas. 2006. Vascular plants utilized by the Plains Apache in southwestern Oklahoma. *Publications of the Oklahoma Biological Survey,* 2nd series, 7:24–33.

Kavanaugh, Thomas W. 2001. Comanche. In *Handbook of North American Indians.* Vol. 13, pt. 2, *Plains,* edited by Raymond J. DeMallie, 886–925. Washington, D.C.: Smithsonian Institution Press.

Kindscher, Kelly. 1987. *Edible wild plants of the prairie: An ethnobotanical guide.* Lawrence: University Press of Kansas.

———. 1992. *Medicinal wild plants of the prairie: An ethnobotanical guide.* Lawrence: University Press of Kansas.

Küchler, A. W. 1964. *Potential natural vegetation of the conterminous United States* [map and manual]. Special Publication 36, American Geographical Society.

La Barre, Weston. 1964. *The peyote cult,* new enlarged edition. Hamden: The Shoe String Press.

Little, Elbert L., Jr. 1998. *Forest trees of Oklahoma: How to know them.* Oklahoma Forestry Services Publication 1, revised edition 15. Oklahoma City: Oklahoma State Department of Agriculture, Forestry Division.

McAllister, J. Gilbert. 1949. Kiowa-Apache tales. In *The sky is my tipi,* edited by Mody C. Boatright, 1–141. Publications of the Texas Folklore Society, 22. Dallas: Texas Folklore Society.

———. 1955. Kiowa-Apache social organization. In *Social anthropology of North American tribes,* 2d ed., edited by Fred Eggan, 97–169. Chicago: University of Chicago Press.

———. 1965. The four quartz rocks medicine bundle of the Kiowa-Apache. *Ethnology* 4:210–24.

———. 1970. *Daveko, Kiowa-Apache medicine man.* Bulletin of the Texas Memorial Museum, vol. 17. Austin: Texas Memorial Museum.

Moerman, Daniel E. 1998. *Native American Ethnobotany.* Portland, Oreg.: Timber Press.

Mooney, James. 1898. Calendar history of the Kiowa Indians. In *17th Annual Report of the Bureau of American Ethnology [for] 1895–96,* part 1, 129–468. Washington, D.C.: Smithsonian Institution; U.S. Government Printing Office.

Newcomb, W. W., Jr. 1970. Summary of Kiowa-Apache history and culture. In *Daveko, Kiowa-Apache medicine man,* by J. Gilbert McAllister, 1–28. Bulletin of the Texas Memorial Museum, vol. 17. Austin: Texas Memorial Museum.

Opler, Morris E. 1983. Chiricahua Apache. In *Handbook of North American Indians.* Vol. 10, *Southwest,* edited by Alfonso Ortiz, 401–18. Washington, D.C.: Smithsonian Institution Press.

Opler, Morris E., and William E. Bittle. 1961. The death practices and eschatology of the Kiowa Apache. *Southwestern Journal of Anthropology* 17:383–94.

Prescott, Philander. 1849. Farming among the Sioux Indians. In *U.S. Patent Office Report on Agriculture,* 451–455.

Schroeder, Albert H. 1974. *A study of the Apache Indians,* vol. 1. New York: Garland Publishing.

Schweinfurth, Kay Parker. 2002. *Prayer on top of the earth: The spiritual universe of the Plains Apaches.* Boulder: University of Colorado Press.

Sims, Phillip L., and Paul G. Risser. 2000. Grassland. In *North American Terrestrial Vegetation,* edited by M. G. Barbour and W. D. Billings, 323–57. Cambridge: Cambridge University Press.

Steyermark, Julian A. 1981 [1963]. *Flora of Missouri.* Ames: Iowa State University Press.

Swagerty, William R. 2001. History of the United States plains until 1850. In *Handbook of North American Indians.* Vol. 13, pt. 1, *Plains,* edited by Raymond J. DeMaillie, 256–79. Washington, D.C.: Smithsonian Institution Press.

United States Department of Agriculture, Natural Resources Conservation Service. 2006. The PLANTS database. http://plants.usda.gov, accessed March 14, 2008.

Vestal, Paul A., and Richard E. Schultes. 1939. *The economic botany of the Kiowa Indians as it relates to the history of the tribe.* Cambridge, Mass.: Botanical Museum of Harvard University.

Wedel, Waldo R. 1959. *An introduction to the archeology of Kansas.* Bureau of American Ethnology Bulletin 174. Washington, D.C.: U.S. Government Printing Office.

———. 1961. *Prehistoric man on the Great Plains.* Norman: University of Oklahoma Press.

Whiting, Alfred F. 1950. Ethnobotany of the Hopi. Museum of Northern Arizona Bulletin 15. Flagstaff, Ariz.: Museum of Northern Arizona.

Wilson, Gilbert L. 1917. *Agriculture of the Hidatsa Indians: An Indian interpretation.* University of Minnesota Studies in the Social Sciences, vol. 9. Minneapolis: University of Minnesota.

Index

www.ingramcontent.com/pod-product-compliance
Lightning Source LLC
Chambersburg PA
CBHW020702270326
41928CB00005B/220